Reality: A Very Short Introduction

VERY SHORT INTRODUCTIONS are for anyone wanting a stimulating and accessible way into a new subject. They are written by experts, and have been translated into more than 45 different languages.

The series began in 1995, and now covers a wide variety of topics in every discipline. The VSI library now contains over 500 volumes—a Very Short Introduction to everything from Psychology and Philosophy of Science to American History and Relativity—and continues to grow in every subject area.

Titles in the series include the following:

AFRICAN HISTORY John Parker and Richard Rathbone
AGEING Nancy A. Pachana
AGNOSTICISM Robin Le Poidevin
AGRICULTURE Paul Brassley and Richard Soffe
ALEXANDER THE GREAT Hugh Bowden
ALGEBRA Peter M. Higgins
AMERICAN HISTORY Paul S. Boyer
AMERICAN IMMIGRATION David A. Gerber
AMERICAN LEGAL HISTORY G. Edward White
AMERICAN POLITICAL HISTORY Donald Critchlow
AMERICAN POLITICAL PARTIES AND ELECTIONS L. Sandy Maisel
AMERICAN POLITICS Richard M. Valelly
THE AMERICAN PRESIDENCY Charles O. Jones
AMERICAN SLAVERY Heather Andrea Williams
THE AMERICAN WEST Stephen Aron
AMERICAN WOMEN'S HISTORY Susan Ware
ANAESTHESIA Aidan O'Donnell
ANARCHISM Colin Ward
ANCIENT EGYPT Ian Shaw
ANCIENT GREECE Paul Cartledge
THE ANCIENT NEAR EAST Amanda H. Podany
ANCIENT PHILOSOPHY Julia Annas
ANCIENT WARFARE Harry Sidebottom
ANGLICANISM Mark Chapman
THE ANGLO-SAXON AGE John Blair
ANIMAL BEHAVIOUR Tristram D. Wyatt
ANIMAL RIGHTS David DeGrazia
ANXIETY Daniel Freeman and Jason Freeman
ARCHAEOLOGY Paul Bahn
ARISTOTLE Jonathan Barnes
ART HISTORY Dana Arnold
ART THEORY Cynthia Freeland
ASTROPHYSICS James Binney
ATHEISM Julian Baggini
THE ATMOSPHERE Paul I. Palmer
AUGUSTINE Henry Chadwick
THE AZTECS Davíd Carrasco
BABYLONIA Trevor Bryce
BACTERIA Sebastian G. B. Amyes
BANKING John Goddard and John O. S. Wilson
BARTHES Jonathan Culler
BEAUTY Roger Scruton
THE BIBLE John Riches
BLACK HOLES Katherine Blundell
BLOOD Chris Cooper
THE BODY Chris Shilling
THE BOOK OF MORMON Terryl Givens
BORDERS Alexander C. Diener and Joshua Hagen
THE BRAIN Michael O'Shea
THE BRICS Andrew F. Cooper
BRITISH POLITICS Anthony Wright

BUDDHA Michael Carrithers
BUDDHISM Damien Keown
BUDDHIST ETHICS Damien Keown
BYZANTIUM Peter Sarris
CANCER Nicholas James
CAPITALISM James Fulcher
CATHOLICISM Gerald O'Collins
CAUSATION Stephen Mumford and Rani Lill Anjum
THE CELL Terence Allen and Graham Cowling
THE CELTS Barry Cunliffe
CHEMISTRY Peter Atkins
CHILD PSYCHOLOGY Usha Goswami
CHINESE LITERATURE Sabina Knight
CHOICE THEORY Michael Allingham
CHRISTIAN ART Beth Williamson
CHRISTIAN ETHICS D. Stephen Long
CHRISTIANITY Linda Woodhead
CIRCADIAN RHYTHMS Russell Foster and Leon Kreitzman
CITIZENSHIP Richard Bellamy
CLASSICAL MYTHOLOGY Helen Morales
CLASSICS Mary Beard and John Henderson
CLIMATE Mark Maslin
CLIMATE CHANGE Mark Maslin
COGNITIVE NEUROSCIENCE Richard Passingham
THE COLD WAR Robert McMahon
COLONIAL AMERICA Alan Taylor
COLONIAL LATIN AMERICAN LITERATURE Rolena Adorno
COMBINATORICS Robin Wilson
COMMUNISM Leslie Holmes
COMPLEXITY John H. Holland
THE COMPUTER Darrel Ince
COMPUTER SCIENCE Subrata Dasgupta
CONFUCIANISM Daniel K. Gardner
CONSCIOUSNESS Susan Blackmore
CONTEMPORARY ART Julian Stallabrass
CONTEMPORARY FICTION Robert Eaglestone
CONTINENTAL PHILOSOPHY Simon Critchley
CORAL REEFS Charles Sheppard
CORPORATE SOCIAL RESPONSIBILITY Jeremy Moon
COSMOLOGY Peter Coles
CRIMINAL JUSTICE Julian V. Roberts
CRITICAL THEORY Stephen Eric Bronner
THE CRUSADES Christopher Tyerman
CRYSTALLOGRAPHY A. M. Glazer
DADA AND SURREALISM David Hopkins
DANTE Peter Hainsworth and David Robey
DARWIN Jonathan Howard
THE DEAD SEA SCROLLS Timothy Lim
DECOLONIZATION Dane Kennedy
DEMOCRACY Bernard Crick
DEPRESSION Jan Scott and Mary Jane Tacchi
DERRIDA Simon Glendinning
DESIGN John Heskett
DEVELOPMENTAL BIOLOGY Lewis Wolpert
DIASPORA Kevin Kenny
DINOSAURS David Norman
DREAMING J. Allan Hobson
DRUGS Les Iversen
DRUIDS Barry Cunliffe
THE EARTH Martin Redfern
EARTH SYSTEM SCIENCE Tim Lenton
ECONOMICS Partha Dasgupta
EGYPTIAN MYTH Geraldine Pinch
EIGHTEENTH-CENTURY BRITAIN Paul Langford
THE ELEMENTS Philip Ball
EMOTION Dylan Evans
EMPIRE Stephen Howe
ENGLISH LITERATURE Jonathan Bate
THE ENLIGHTENMENT John Robertson
ENVIRONMENTAL ECONOMICS Stephen Smith
ENVIRONMENTAL POLITICS Andrew Dobson
EPICUREANISM Catherine Wilson
EPIDEMIOLOGY Rodolfo Saracci
ETHICS Simon Blackburn
THE ETRUSCANS Christopher Smith
EUGENICS Philippa Levine
THE EUROPEAN UNION John Pinder and Simon Usherwood
EVOLUTION Brian and Deborah Charlesworth

EXISTENTIALISM Thomas Flynn
THE EYE Michael Land
FAMILY LAW Jonathan Herring
FASCISM Kevin Passmore
FEMINISM Margaret Walters
FILM Michael Wood
FILM MUSIC Kathryn Kalinak
THE FIRST WORLD WAR Michael Howard
FOOD John Krebs
FORENSIC PSYCHOLOGY David Canter
FORENSIC SCIENCE Jim Fraser
FORESTS Jaboury Ghazoul
FOSSILS Keith Thomson
FOUCAULT Gary Gutting
FREE SPEECH Nigel Warburton
FREE WILL Thomas Pink
FREUD Anthony Storr
FUNDAMENTALISM Malise Ruthven
FUNGI Nicholas P. Money
THE FUTURE Jennifer M. Gidley
GALAXIES John Gribbin
GALILEO Stillman Drake
GAME THEORY Ken Binmore
GANDHI Bhikhu Parekh
GEOGRAPHY John Matthews and David Herbert
GEOPOLITICS Klaus Dodds
GERMAN LITERATURE Nicholas Boyle
GERMAN PHILOSOPHY Andrew Bowie
GLOBAL CATASTROPHES Bill McGuire
GLOBAL ECONOMIC HISTORY Robert C. Allen
GLOBALIZATION Manfred Steger
GOD John Bowker
GRAVITY Timothy Clifton
THE GREAT DEPRESSION AND THE NEW DEAL Eric Rauchway
HABERMAS James Gordon Finlayson
THE HEBREW BIBLE AS LITERATURE Tod Linafelt
HEGEL Peter Singer
HERODOTUS Jennifer T. Roberts
HIEROGLYPHS Penelope Wilson
HINDUISM Kim Knott
HISTORY John H. Arnold
THE HISTORY OF ASTRONOMY Michael Hoskin
THE HISTORY OF CHEMISTRY William H. Brock
THE HISTORY OF LIFE Michael Benton
THE HISTORY OF MATHEMATICS Jacqueline Stedall
THE HISTORY OF MEDICINE William Bynum
THE HISTORY OF TIME Leofranc Holford-Strevens
HIV AND AIDS Alan Whiteside
HOLLYWOOD Peter Decherney
HUMAN ANATOMY Leslie Klenerman
HUMAN EVOLUTION Bernard Wood
HUMAN RIGHTS Andrew Clapham
THE ICE AGE Jamie Woodward
IDEOLOGY Michael Freeden
INDIAN PHILOSOPHY Sue Hamilton
THE INDUSTRIAL REVOLUTION Robert C. Allen
INFECTIOUS DISEASE Marta L. Wayne and Benjamin M. Bolker
INFINITY Ian Stewart
INFORMATION Luciano Floridi
INNOVATION Mark Dodgson and David Gann
INTELLIGENCE Ian J. Deary
INTERNATIONAL MIGRATION Khalid Koser
INTERNATIONAL RELATIONS Paul Wilkinson
IRAN Ali M. Ansari
ISLAM Malise Ruthven
ISLAMIC HISTORY Adam Silverstein
ISOTOPES Rob Ellam
ITALIAN LITERATURE Peter Hainsworth and David Robey
JESUS Richard Bauckham
JOURNALISM Ian Hargreaves
JUDAISM Norman Solomon
JUNG Anthony Stevens
KABBALAH Joseph Dan
KANT Roger Scruton
KNOWLEDGE Jennifer Nagel
THE KORAN Michael Cook
LATE ANTIQUITY Gillian Clark
LAW Raymond Wacks
THE LAWS OF THERMODYNAMICS Peter Atkins
LEADERSHIP Keith Grint
LEARNING Mark Haselgrove

LEIBNIZ Maria Rosa Antognazza
LIBERALISM Michael Freeden
LIGHT Ian Walmsley
LINGUISTICS Peter Matthews
LITERARY THEORY Jonathan Culler
LOCKE John Dunn
LOGIC Graham Priest
MACHIAVELLI Quentin Skinner
MAGIC Owen Davies
MAGNA CARTA Nicholas Vincent
MAGNETISM Stephen Blundell
MARINE BIOLOGY Philip V. Mladenov
MARTIN LUTHER Scott H. Hendrix
MARTYRDOM Jolyon Mitchell
MARX Peter Singer
MATERIALS Christopher Hall
MATHEMATICS Timothy Gowers
THE MEANING OF LIFE Terry Eagleton
MEASUREMENT David Hand
MEDICAL ETHICS Tony Hope
MEDIEVAL BRITAIN John Gillingham and Ralph A. Griffiths
MEDIEVAL LITERATURE Elaine Treharne
MEDIEVAL PHILOSOPHY John Marenbon
MEMORY Jonathan K. Foster
METAPHYSICS Stephen Mumford
MICROBIOLOGY Nicholas P. Money
MICROECONOMICS Avinash Dixit
MICROSCOPY Terence Allen
THE MIDDLE AGES Miri Rubin
MILITARY JUSTICE Eugene R. Fidell
MINERALS David Vaughan
MODERN ART David Cottington
MODERN CHINA Rana Mitter
MODERN FRANCE Vanessa R. Schwartz
MODERN IRELAND Senia Pašeta
MODERN ITALY Anna Cento Bull
MODERN JAPAN Christopher Goto-Jones
MODERNISM Christopher Butler
MOLECULAR BIOLOGY Aysha Divan and Janice A. Royds
MOLECULES Philip Ball
MOONS David A. Rothery
MOUNTAINS Martin F. Price
MUHAMMAD Jonathan A. C. Brown
MUSIC Nicholas Cook
MYTH Robert A. Segal
THE NAPOLEONIC WARS Mike Rapport
NELSON MANDELA Elleke Boehmer
NEOLIBERALISM Manfred Steger and Ravi Roy
NEWTON Robert Iliffe
NIETZSCHE Michael Tanner
NINETEENTH-CENTURY BRITAIN Christopher Harvie and H. C. G. Matthew
NORTH AMERICAN INDIANS Theda Perdue and Michael D. Green
NORTHERN IRELAND Marc Mulholland
NOTHING Frank Close
NUCLEAR PHYSICS Frank Close
NUMBERS Peter M. Higgins
NUTRITION David A. Bender
THE OLD TESTAMENT Michael D. Coogan
ORGANIC CHEMISTRY Graham Patrick
THE PALESTINIAN-ISRAELI CONFLICT Martin Bunton
PANDEMICS Christian W. McMillen
PARTICLE PHYSICS Frank Close
THE PERIODIC TABLE Eric R. Scerri
PHILOSOPHY Edward Craig
PHILOSOPHY IN THE ISLAMIC WORLD Peter Adamson
PHILOSOPHY OF LAW Raymond Wacks
PHILOSOPHY OF SCIENCE Samir Okasha
PHOTOGRAPHY Steve Edwards
PHYSICAL CHEMISTRY Peter Atkins
PILGRIMAGE Ian Reader
PLAGUE Paul Slack
PLANETS David A. Rothery
PLANTS Timothy Walker
PLATE TECTONICS Peter Molnar
PLATO Julia Annas
POLITICAL PHILOSOPHY David Miller
POLITICS Kenneth Minogue
POPULISM Cas Mudde and Cristóbal Rovira Kaltwasser
POSTCOLONIALISM Robert Young

POSTMODERNISM Christopher Butler
POSTSTRUCTURALISM
Catherine Belsey
PREHISTORY Chris Gosden
PRESOCRATIC PHILOSOPHY
Catherine Osborne
PRIVACY Raymond Wacks
PSYCHIATRY Tom Burns
PSYCHOLOGY Gillian Butler and
Freda McManus
PSYCHOTHERAPY Tom Burns and
Eva Burns-Lundgren
PUBLIC ADMINISTRATION
Stella Z. Theodoulou and Ravi K. Roy
PUBLIC HEALTH Virginia Berridge
QUANTUM THEORY
John Polkinghorne
RACISM Ali Rattansi
REALITY Jan Westerhoff
THE REFORMATION Peter Marshall
RELATIVITY Russell Stannard
RELIGION IN AMERICA Timothy Beal
THE RENAISSANCE Jerry Brotton
RENAISSANCE ART
Geraldine A. Johnson
REVOLUTIONS Jack A. Goldstone
RHETORIC Richard Toye
RISK Baruch Fischhoff and John Kadvany
RITUAL Barry Stephenson
RIVERS Nick Middleton
ROBOTICS Alan Winfield
ROMAN BRITAIN Peter Salway
THE ROMAN EMPIRE Christopher Kelly
THE ROMAN REPUBLIC
David M. Gwynn
RUSSIAN HISTORY Geoffrey Hosking
RUSSIAN LITERATURE Catriona Kelly
THE RUSSIAN REVOLUTION
S. A. Smith
SAVANNAS Peter A. Furley
SCHIZOPHRENIA Chris Frith and
Eve Johnstone
SCIENCE AND RELIGION
Thomas Dixon
THE SCIENTIFIC REVOLUTION
Lawrence M. Principe
SCOTLAND Rab Houston
SEXUALITY Véronique Mottier
SHAKESPEARE'S COMEDIES Bart van Es
SIKHISM Eleanor Nesbitt
SLEEP Steven W. Lockley and
Russell G. Foster
SOCIAL AND CULTURAL
ANTHROPOLOGY
John Monaghan and Peter Just
SOCIAL PSYCHOLOGY Richard J. Crisp
SOCIAL WORK Sally Holland and
Jonathan Scourfield
SOCIALISM Michael Newman
SOCIOLOGY Steve Bruce
SOCRATES C. C. W. Taylor
SOUND Mike Goldsmith
THE SOVIET UNION Stephen Lovell
THE SPANISH CIVIL WAR
Helen Graham
SPANISH LITERATURE Jo Labanyi
SPORT Mike Cronin
STARS Andrew King
STATISTICS David J. Hand
STUART BRITAIN John Morrill
SYMMETRY Ian Stewart
TAXATION Stephen Smith
TELESCOPES Geoff Cottrell
TERRORISM Charles Townshend
THEOLOGY David F. Ford
TIBETAN BUDDHISM
Matthew T. Kapstein
THE TROJAN WAR Eric H. Cline
THE TUDORS John Guy
TWENTIETH-CENTURY BRITAIN
Kenneth O. Morgan
THE UNITED NATIONS
Jussi M. Hanhimäki
THE U.S. CONGRESS Donald A. Ritchie
THE U.S. SUPREME COURT
Linda Greenhouse
THE VIKINGS Julian Richards
VIRUSES Dorothy H. Crawford
VOLTAIRE Nicholas Cronk
WAR AND TECHNOLOGY
Alex Roland
WATER John Finney
WILLIAM SHAKESPEARE
Stanley Wells
WITCHCRAFT Malcolm Gaskill
THE WORLD TRADE
ORGANIZATION Amrita Narlikar
WORLD WAR II Gerhard L. Weinberg

Jan Westerhoff

# REALITY

## A Very Short Introduction

OXFORD
UNIVERSITY PRESS

Great Clarendon Street, Oxford OX2 6DP

Oxford University Press is a department of the University of Oxford.
It furthers the University's objective of excellence in research, scholarship,
and education by publishing worldwide in

Oxford New York

Auckland Cape Town Dar es Salaam Hong Kong Karachi
Kuala Lumpur Madrid Melbourne Mexico City Nairobi
New Delhi Shanghai Taipei Toronto

With offices in

Argentina Austria Brazil Chile Czech Republic France Greece
Guatemala Hungary Italy Japan Poland Portugal Singapore
South Korea Switzerland Thailand Turkey Ukraine Vietnam

Oxford is a registered trade mark of Oxford University Press
in the UK and in certain other countries

Published in the United States
by Oxford University Press Inc., New York



First published 2011



British Library Cataloguing in Publication Data
Data available

Library of Congress Cataloging in Publication Data
Data available

Typeset by SPI Publisher Services, Pondicherry, India
Printed and bound by
CPI Group (UK) Ltd, Croydon, CR0 4YY

ISBN 978–0–19–959441–2

# Contents

# List of illustrations

# Introduction

As you are standing here (perhaps in a bookshop, or a library, or at home), reading this page, you probably believe that the book, the paper it is printed on, and the letters on the page are real. You are not just dreaming that you hold this book and read this sentence, you are really doing so. You most likely also believe that *you* are real, that you are not just dreamt up by somebody (like Alice is dreamt by the Red King) dreaming about somebody reading a book on reality. This reflects a healthy psychological attitude. Most people do not believe they are dreaming most of the time (very few people believe they are dreaming when they are in fact doing so), do not assume that the material objects around them aren't really there, and do not believe they are a character in someone else's novel. Yet never to have at least suspected whether things might not be exactly this way suggests a lack of philosophical imagination.

In this book, we will look at some arguments supporting such suspicions, and we will try to find out whether these arguments are good arguments. In the first chapter, we will ask how (if at all) we could tell our waking experiences from dreams and simulations. This is followed by looking at the question of whether the material objects around us, such as books, tables, and chairs, are real. Chapter 3 asks the question whether persons are real, and in particular whether you, the reader of this book, are real. The final chapter considers the reality of time, the medium in which you and all the objects around you apparently exist.

# Chapter 1
# Dreams and simulations

One night, the French zoologist Yves Delage is woken up by a knock on the door. It is the caretaker, telling him to get up as a friend has fallen ill. Delage gets out of bed, dresses, and quickly walks into his dressing room to wash his face with a wet sponge. The sensation of cold water wakes him up: he is in fact lying in bed, undressed, there was no one knocking at the door. The whole experience has been a dream.

Minutes later, there is another knock at the door. It is the caretaker: 'Monsieur, aren't you coming then?' 'Good heavens! So it is really true! I thought I had dreamt it.' 'Not at all. Hurry up, they are all waiting for you!' Delage gets up, dresses, hurries to the dressing room to wash his face. When his face makes contact with the sponge, he wakes up, undressed, in bed. After a short while, there is another knock, and again, the caretaker: 'Monsieur...'.

The whole sequence, we are told, repeated itself four times before Delage finally wakes up in the real world. Delage experienced the unusual but not rare phenomenon of *false awakening*: he woke up into what he thought was the real world, only to realize that this, too, was a dream. Waking up again, it turns out that he is still in a dream from which he has yet to awake. The number of layers dreamers go through before finally waking up can be quite large, and those experiencing false awakenings often find the whole process very distressing.

There are two main reasons for this. The first is the horror of being stuck in a cycle of the eternal return of the same, a kind of internal *Groundhog Day* in which events are replayed *ad infinitum*. The second is the suspicion false awakenings can give us concerning the reality of true awakenings. Awakening from one dream into another one, 'one level further down', felt completely real and convincing – so how do we know that the awakening we experienced this morning just before getting out of bed was a real awakening? How do you know that you didn't just wake up into another dream, one that contains all the experiences you are presently having, and that in a short while you will awake again, either into the waking world or into yet another dream?



Contemplating the possibility that you are dreaming right now is certainly very perplexing. You might think that it is also exceedingly unlikely, something in the same ballpark as hitting the jackpot in a lottery or suddenly dropping dead. There are various things that are theoretically possible, even though their probability is very low (such as a monkey randomly hitting on a typewriter writing out the complete works of Shakespeare, or the sudden disappearance of objects due to an effect called 'quantum tunnelling'). If you don't worry that this book might suddenly disappear from your hands due to some bizarre quantum effect, why worry that you might be dreaming right now?

The reason why you should worry is that the chances of you dreaming at this very moment are far, far greater. Let's do a quick calculation. We optimistically assume that you get eight hours of sleep a night, which leaves sixteen hours during which you are awake. Sleep researchers have found out that there is a strong correlation between dreaming and being in so-called REM (rapid eye movement) sleep. REM sleep is characterized by rapid movement of the eyeballs; the brain is highly active, its electric

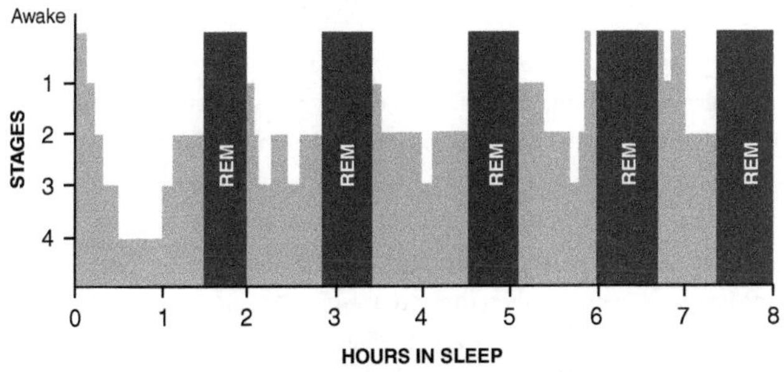

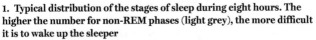

**1. Typical distribution of the stages of sleep during eight hours. The higher the number for non-REM phases (light grey), the more difficult it is to wake up the sleeper**



activity resembles that of a waking brain, but the sleeper is more difficult to wake than during slow-wave or non-REM sleep. We know that between 20% and 25% of our sleep is REM sleep. Taking the lower value and assuming that you always and only dream during REM sleep, this gives us 1.6 hours of dreaming every night. As there are therefore 1.6 hours of dream consciousness for every 16 hours of waking consciousness, this means that your chance of dreaming at any given moment is 1 in 10. This quite a high probability – for comparison: the chance of winning the jackpot of a typical lottery is about 1 in 14 millions (this means that if you bought a ticket every week, you would have one win on average every 250,000 years); the chance of the author of this book dying in an accident within the next year is somewhat less than 1 in 2,500.

So there is a significant chance of you dreaming right now. But does it matter? To be sure, we can't exclude the possibility that this is all a dream, but as long as it continues, it will not make the slightest difference to how we lead our lives. Even if the £5 note in my pocket is just dream-money, and the strawberry cake I buy with it is only a dream-cake, I can still have the sensation of eating the strawberry cake as a result, and what more can I want? Even if I am dreaming

### How fast does time pass in a dream?

Does time flow at the same rate when we are dreaming as when we are awake? Anecdotal evidence seems to suggest that it can flow considerably faster. The prophet Muhammad famously visited the seven heavens in a dream that took less time than water flowing out of an upturned pitcher. Many of us have dreams involving plots lasting for several days and therefore appear to be considerably longer than the actual amount of time we spent dreaming. If this was true, there would be more moments of consciousness for every unit of sleeping time we spend dreaming, so that the chance of dreaming right now would be considerably larger than 0.1. However, research into lucid dreaming (that is, dreams in which the dreamer knows she is dreaming) has shown that time passes at about the same rate in a dream as it does in waking life. When lucid dreamers move the eyeballs of their dream bodies, this causes their real eyeballs to move as well. Such movement can be tracked in a sleep laboratory, and dreamers can thereby send signals from dreams to the waking world. For example, subjects can be asked to move their eyes five times from left to right in a lucid dream, estimate a period of time, and then move them again. Real time and dream time can now be compared. Experiments showed that on average an estimated duration of 10 seconds lasts 13 seconds while we are awake; this is the same amount of time it takes during a lucid dream. It appears that waking experience and dreams contain the same number of moments of consciousness per unit of waking time.

right now, I will still be able to plan my life, cause will follow effect, and actions will have consequences. Of course, these consequences will just be dream-consequences, but given that we have assumed earlier that I would not be able to tell ‘from the inside’ whether I am dreaming or not, why should I worry about this? The world of experiences is still the same, and this is all that counts, after all.

But this reasoning is a bit too quick. In fact, it would make a considerable difference if you were dreaming right now. For starters, the greatest part of your beliefs would be false. You might believe there is a piece of strawberry cake out there, a material object, produced by a baker, that has a certain shape, weight, sugar content, and causes your perception of this piece of cake. All of this would be false. There would be no cake with its properties, just a set of images in your mind that are put together in a specific way to form your idea of a piece of cake, without any connection with an external cake at all.

Secondly, you would probably have to revise your beliefs about ethics and morality. You may think that there are people around you, your spouse, your parents, friends, and colleagues. In a dream, none of this is true. There are ideas in your mind that you think represent people, but in fact they don't. Now we usually think we should act morally because of the consequences our actions have for other people. If some act causes suffering for others, we should refrain from doing it; if it causes their happiness, we should strive to do it. But if all the people you interact with are just images in your dream, this entire motivation falls away. You should still avoid immoral actions that have unpleasant consequences for *you* (ending up in a dream-prison is, after all, not any better than ending up in a real prison), but as long as you can get away with it, the wishes and concerns of other beings need not deter you from any action, since these wishes and concerns are wholly unreal.



So there are in fact substantial consequences for what you know and for how you should act if all your experience is a dream. These consequences become particularly extreme if we assume that all that exists is just you and the ideas in your mind. This philosophical position is known as *solipsism* and shrinks the world to the size of your mind. (You might know the joke about a confused solipsist writing to an agony aunt: 'Dear Madam, I am a solipsist. This is an admirable position to be in and I wonder why there are not more of them.') Compared to solipsism, the belief that you are currently dreaming is quite mild. If you are dreaming right now, there will also be a time when you wake up, and there is a limited way in which we could say that you may have some true beliefs (perhaps beliefs in the truths of mathematics, which may also hold in the waking world). We might also make an argument for moral behaviour in the dream-world (if we say that immoral behaviour deforms your character, and if your character is something that is at least partly present in your waking state). But for a solipsist, *there is no outside world*, there are no things, and no people. There is just one person, me, and everything that happens in my mind.

The worry whether we are dreaming right now is commonly associated with the French philosopher René Descartes (1596–1650) who discusses it at the beginning of his *Meditations on First Philosophy*. In the contemporary discussion, this worry is often investigated by considering its more modern and high-tech variant: the worry that we might be a brain in a vat.



Modern medical technology allows us to keep alive human beings lacking a variety of vital organs, such as the heart or the kidneys. Soon, there will be functional artificial lungs and livers, and it is not too much of a stretch of the imagination to suggest that at some time in the future we will be able to sustain the life of a human brain even though its body has been destroyed. Such a brain will be supplied with nutrients via a blood substitute, usually an oxygenated solution of various salts, and would no longer be dependent on its former body for life-sustaining functions. Success in this direction has been achieved with the brains of guinea-pigs, and it seems to be only a matter of time before medical science can do the same with the brains of humans.

The main difficulty, however, is not how to keep such a brain alive, but how to keep it stimulated. After all, being such an artificially

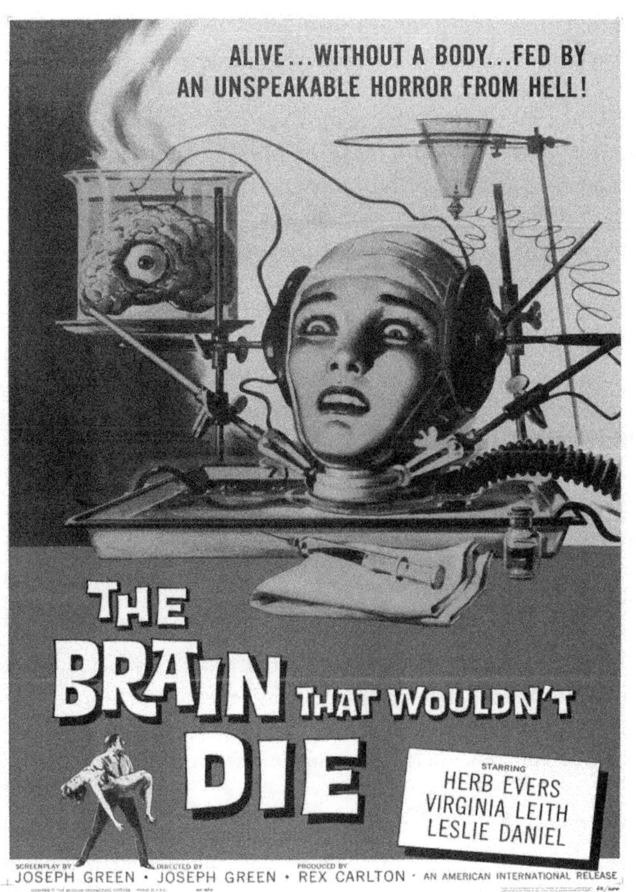


**2. Early cinematic adaptation of the brain-in-a-vat scenario**

sustained isolated brain would be like being simultaneously paralysed, blind, deaf, mute, unable to smell, taste, or touch. This would be a worse state to be in than the so-called 'locked-in' patients who are fully paralysed and unable to move or communicate due to damage of the lower brain and brainstem.

At least, these patients receive some perceptual input, but an isolated brain does not obtain any information about the world around it. To keep a brain in a jar happy, it would therefore be a good idea to stimulate its nerves in a way that simulates input from its former sensory organs. Doing this in any comprehensive manner is definitely beyond the abilities of present-day science, but the basics of the necessary technology are available. Brain–computer interfaces have been used to restore limited sight to the non-congenitally blind by implanting a set of electrodes linked to a camera directly into their visual cortex, and similarly encouraging results have been obtained with robotic arms. In the future, descendants of these technologies might allow us to provide entire simulated worlds for the entertainment of isolated brains on life support. Of course, these simulated worlds would not be close to the way the world actually is. It would strike us as downright cruel to send electric impulses into the brain that let it see what it would see if it still had eyes attached to it: the inside of a jar filled with a liquid nutrient, and beyond that the depressing sight of the Isolated Brain Support Unit of the local hospital, filled with shelves housing rows upon rows of fellow brains. As the simulated reality is part of a medical treatment with the purpose to reduce the patient's suffering, would it not be much better to give her (or rather her brain) a simulated world in which she still has a body and is a happy human leading a fulfilled life in every sense?

But this raises a disquieting thought: if that is what doctors would do, and if the necessary technological tools will be available at some point, *how do we know this is not happening to us already?* It is no good to reply 'We live at the beginning of the 21st century, and doctors are not able to do this yet.' If we are an isolated brain supplied with a simulated world, it may well be the case that it seems to be the year 2011 in the simulated world, but the real date is 2199. Deceiving you about the date may be part of the therapeutic plan: perhaps the world of 2199 is an upsetting and not very nice place to live in. You are much better off experiencing a simulated 2011.

You might think such world-simulations are not really feasible. After all, to be realistic, the simulators would not just have to present the brain with a world that apparently cannot be changed (something like making the brain watch a neuronal movie), but with a world it can interact with, a world it can influence by the decisions it makes (something closer to making the brain play a neuronal computer game). So if you walk down a simulated street and suddenly decide to open a door of one of the houses, the simulators would instantly have to supply everything you would be seeing, hearing, touching, smelling, or tasting in the house. Constructing such a vast amount of simulated reality and supplying it to the brain in real time is a formidable task that is not just beyond our present technological abilities, but might be beyond those of any future civilization as well.

Unfortunately, this is not a very convincing argument against the possibility of you being a brain in a jar. First of all, your simulators can be placed arbitrarily far in the future, at times that compare to the 21st century as the present compares to the stone age. Computers at that time might well be able to tackle the 'combinatorial explosion' caused by having to simulate in response to an agent's choice. Or perhaps, and this is the second point, such vast computational resources might not be necessary. Our brain is fairly complex, but its computational power is not that large. Estimates range between a hundred teraflops (one teraflop is $10^{12}$ operations per second) and a thousand times as much, a hundred petaflops. The first supercomputer with a theoretical peak performance of a hundred teraflops, the ASCI Purple, was installed in 2005. The current number one on the list of supercomputers, the Cray Jaguar, has a maximal capacity of 1.75 petaflops. If Moore's law predicting the doubling of computing power every two years continues to hold, we'll be getting at a hundred petaflops in little more than a decade. Such a computer would have the resources to produce a convincing world-simulation, for the simple reason that our computationally equivalent brains do so every night when we are dreaming.

As 'just-in-time' simulation appears to be no great problem for our own brains, the difficulties involved are presumably not insurmountable.

Is there any way of removing the disquieting suspicion that we are artificially animated brains deluded by computer-generated world-simulations? If true, the suspicion should indeed make us nervous. What do we know about the moral standards of the scientists manipulating our brains? Do they have our best interests at heart? If not, how do we know the simulation won't suddenly become incoherent (perhaps due to a bug in the simulation program) or, worse, turn nasty (since an evil scientist is placing our brain in his favourite horror movie)? In fact, do we even know there is a scientist at the other end of our brain? There may just be a giant computer running the simulation, and this, together with the brains, could be all there is in the universe.



But there seems to be something wrong with this whole idea. To see what, consider first of all that beliefs refer to what caused them. If I think there is a banana in front of me, there is a chain of causes that can be traced back from the idea in my mind, via some neuronal activity in my brain, excitation of photo-receptive cells in my retina, and reflected light-waves all the way to the banana. And if there isn't a suitable chain of causes like this, there is no reference, even though it might still *look* as if there was. If I write 'Joe' in my diary to remind myself to send him a birthday card, 'Joe' refers to Joe because there is a causal chain going back all the way to Joe, as there is in the case of the banana. But if drop my Scrabble board, and three of the tiles that land on the floor happen to spell 'JOE', they do not refer to my friend.

In 1923, the face of Henry Liddell, Dean of Christ Church at Oxford University and father of Alice (the real-life model of Lewis Carroll's *Alice in Wonderland*) appeared in the drying mortar of the wall just below the memorial window set up for him in Christ Church Cathedral. Even though there appear to be no

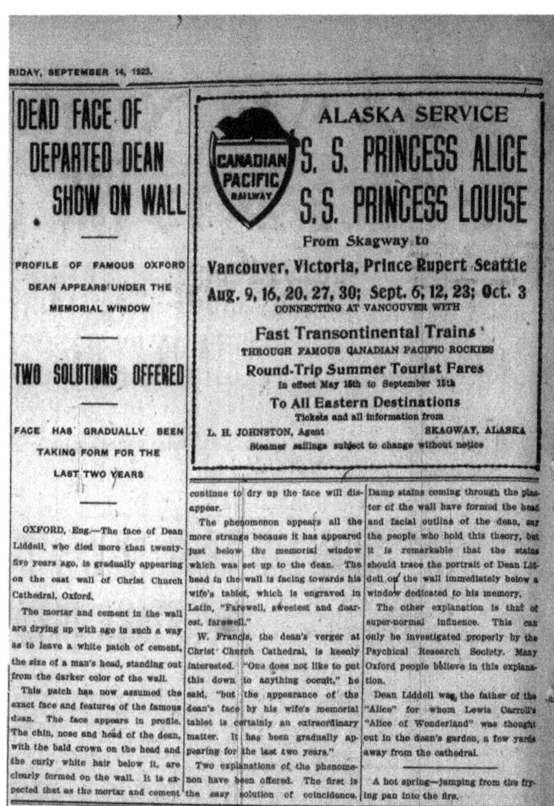

RIDAY, SEPTEMBER 14, 1923.

**DEAD FACE OF DEPARTED DEAN SHOW ON WALL**

PROFILE OF FAMOUS OXFORD DEAN APPEARS UNDER THE MEMORIAL WINDOW

**TWO SOLUTIONS OFFERED**

FACE HAS GRADUALLY BEEN TAKING FORM FOR THE LAST TWO YEARS

OXFORD, Eng.—The face of Dean Liddell, who died more than twenty-five years ago, is gradually appearing on the east wall of Christ Church Cathedral, Oxford.

The mortar and cement in the wall are drying up with age in such a way as to leave a white patch of cement, the size of a man's head, standing out from the darker color of the wall.

This patch has now assumed the exact face and features of the famous dean. The face appears in profile. The chin, nose and head of the dean, with the bald crown on the head and the curly white hair below it, are clearly formed on the wall. It is expected that as the mortar and cement continue to dry up the face will disappear.

The phenomenon appears all the more strange because it has appeared just below the memorial window which was set up to the dean. The head in the wall is facing towards his wife's tablet, which is engraved in Latin, "Farewell, sweetest and dearest, farewell."

W. Francis, the dean's verger at Christ Church Cathedral, is keenly interested. "One does not like to put this down to anything occult," he said, "but the appearance of the dean's face by his wife's memorial tablet is certainly an extraordinary matter. It has been gradually appearing for the last two years."

Two explanations of the phenomenon have been offered. The first is the easy solution of coincidence. Damp stains coming through the plaster of the wall have formed the head and facial outline of the dean, say the people who hold this theory, but it is remarkable that the stains should trace the portrait of Dean Liddell on the wall immediately below a window dedicated to his memory.

The other explanation is that of super-normal influence. This can only be investigated properly by the Psychical Research Society. Many Oxford people believe in this explanation.

Dean Liddell was the father of the "Alice" for whom Lewis Carroll's "Alice of Wonderland" was thought out in the dean's garden, a few yards away from the cathedral.

A hot spring—jumping from the frying pan into the fire.



**3.** ***Dawson Daily News*** **reporting the mysterious appearance of Dean Liddell's portrait on the wall of Christ Church Cathedral**

photographs, contemporary accounts assure us that 'the chin, nose and head of the dean, with the bald crown on the head and the curly white hair below it, are clearly formed on the wall'. Given that there is no more of a causal chain linking the patches on the wall to the dead dean than linking 'JOE' to the actual person, the patches do not represent Henry Liddell, even though it may appear as if they did.

Now assume the simulation provided for some brain gives it the belief it is standing in front of the Taj Mahal. What does its idea 'Taj Mahal' refer to? Not to the building, since there is no such thing in the universe. (Remember that we have a universe in which there are just brains in their jars, plus a computer running the show, and nothing else.) Given that beliefs refer to what caused them, and given that this brain's belief was caused by a piece of code contained in the simulation provided by the giant computer, the brain's idea 'Taj Mahal' refers to a piece of computer code! And this has the somewhat surprising consequence that most of this brain's beliefs are actually true. If it believes that the Taj Mahal was built by Shah Jahan, it believes that the Taj Mahal (a piece of computer code) is related to Shah Jahan (another piece of computer code) in a certain way – and this is indeed how it is, since they are related in this way in the code underlying the simulation. Similarly, if, given the simulation provided, the brain thinks 'I'm standing in front of the Taj Mahal', it is not deluded, even though there is no body, and there is no Taj Mahal. This is because, even though there is nothing *our* idea 'body' and our idea 'Taj Mahal' refers to in this universe, there is something that *the brain's* ideas refer to. What causes our idea of the Taj Mahal does not exist in this universe, but what causes theirs, and therefore, what their idea refers to, does exist.



Let us distinguish what the brain's ideas refer to (i.e. the pieces of computer code) by writing it in **bold**, so that we can say that our idea of the Taj Mahal refers to the Taj Mahal, but their idea of the Taj Mahal refers to the **Taj Mahal**.

Now assume you are just a brain in the universe just described. If you are a brain in a simulation, your idea 'brain' does not refer to a brain (it rather refers to a **brain**) and your idea 'simulation' does not refer to a simulation (but to a **simulation**). But if your belief that you are a brain in a simulation does not refer to a brain, then the belief is false, in the same way as your belief that yetis are vegetarian is false if it does not refer to yetis (for example, if there are no yetis). So if you are a brain in a simulation, then your belief that you are a brain in a simulation is false.

Something has gone wrong here. Surely if you are a brain in a simulation, your belief that you are should be *true* (in the same way as the belief that you are overweight should be true if you were twice your actual weight). Yet the opposite is the case.

The problem seems to be that the words, ideas, and beliefs of the brain provided with the simulation and our words, ideas, and beliefs are strictly isolated from each other. Our talk refers to whatever is the cause of our ideas, and their talk refers to whatever is the cause of their ideas, and these causes are very different things. To ask the question whether *we* could happen to be in *their* world, we would have to have a language that includes both, that is a language based on ideas caused both by things like shoes, ships, and sealing-wax, and by ideas caused by **shoes**, **ships**, and **sealing-wax**. But if we can use this language, then we can't be brains in a world in which there are just brains and the giant computer, since shoes, ships, and sealing-wax won't have any causal influences there. They simply do not exist in such a world. In which case, we might wonder: 'If we can't even coherently *describe* the possibility that we are just electrically stimulated brains, why worry about it?'

Unfortunately, this does not get us very far in ruling out the possibility that we are brains in a simulation. First of all, there are various difficulties with the argument just presented. Of course, I can't talk using words that don't refer, but I can talk about things that don't exist by using words that do refer. I can perfectly well talk about yetis, even if there are none, by taking 'yeti' to mean 'large, apelike creature inhabiting the Himalayas'. All of these terms refer, there is just nothing, we assume, that they collectively pick out. Similarly, can't the brain and I use ideas in our respective languages that do refer, to think about things that don't exist in our worlds, such as real trees, or bits of computer code that cause highly realistic and detailed impressions of trees? At least, nothing in the above argument shows that they cannot.

A greater difficulty, however, is that the argument just given only manages to rule out a very specific case, even if it is successful. Even if we grant that we cannot coherently describe a world in which there are only artificially stimulated brains, what about other, closely related scenarios? Suppose last night evil scientists removed your brain from your body, kept it alive in a high-tech Brain Support Unit, and simulated exactly those experiences you are currently having (that is, the experience of reading this sentence)? Note that in this case, your ideas wouldn't suddenly refer to something different, as in the example just described. Of course, your experience of seeing the Taj Mahal would now be caused by a piece of computer code run by the Brain Support Unit. But you are still in a world in which the Taj Mahal exists, and the chain of causes that bring about your experience can be traced beyond the computer code to the programmer who wrote the code, to the photos of the Taj Mahal he used to create a simulation of it, to the photographer who took the photos, and, finally, to the Taj Mahal itself. So your idea of the Taj Mahal still refers to the real thing, rather than to the **Taj Mahal**. The ideas, beliefs, and words of normal human beings are not isolated from those of the electrically stimulated brain. As such, we cannot simply argue that even the description of such a scenario is incoherent. We might then reasonably ask what the advantage of an argument ruling out the 'only brains and a computer in the universe' scenario is, if there are so many other scenarios (such as the 'all male brains have been removed by evil female scientists' scenario, the 'all human brains have been removed by aliens' scenario, and so on) that are left untouched as real possibilities.

Finally, we have to note that the conclusion our argument arrived at was only that the 'only brains and a computer in the universe' scenario could not be coherently described. But this does not show that such a scenario could not exist. We might instead understand this argument as showing that there are some possible situations I could be in, but that I lack even the conceptual resources to describe them. Like some menacing Rumsfeldian unknown unknown, these possibilities are out there, and I might be in one of them, but I can't even get a clear enough grip of them to determine how likely or unlikely this would be. Far from alleviating our worrying suspicion that we might be artificially stimulated brains, the argument has actually made matters worse, for we now don't just have to worry about all the unpleasant possibilities we can think of, but also about those we could not possibly think of.

We might think that the possibility that you are dreaming right now, that you are a disembodied brain in an artificial simulated environment, or any other outlandish possibility we can think of, leaves one truth untouched: that it is you who is experiencing this, and that you, the experiencer, are real. You might be mistaken in various ways about who you are (mistaken about whether you are old or young, whether you are male or female, whether you have a body at all), but you cannot be mistaken about your own existence. After all, there cannot be an illusion without somebody having the illusion. This certainty might not be much, but it is something. In fact, René Descartes thought that it was good enough to build his entire philosophical system on the certainty of existence while doubting his existence, since there cannot be a doubt without somebody who does the doubting. Unfortunately, there are interesting arguments that the certainty about our own existence, like the certainty about the existence of the external world, might turn out to be illusory.

It is a well-known fact that the self we experience in dreams has very different properties from our waking self. It does not have access to many of the waking self's memories, usually has a different set of predominant emotions (often more negative ones), it may have a different body, or even a body of a different gender. Given these significant differences, could there possibly be a dream in which the main character was not you, even though her experiences are part of

### 'The Circular Ruins'

In the short story 'The Circular Ruins', Jorge Luis Borges describes a magician, probably from ancient Bactria, who dreams a young man into existence. The God of Fire helps him to animate his creation, and also makes this phantom invulnerable to flames. This is how the story ends:

> After a certain time, which some chronicles prefer to compute in years and others in decades, two oarsmen awoke him at midnight; he could not see their faces, but they spoke to him of a charmed man in a temple of the North, capable of walking on fire without burning himself. The magician suddenly remembered the words of the god. He remembered that of all the creatures that people the earth, Fire was the only one who knew his son to be a phantom. This memory, which at first calmed him, ended by tormenting him. He feared lest his son should meditate on this abnormal privilege and by some means find out he was a mere simulacrum. Not to be a man, to be a projection of another man's dreams – what an incomparable humiliation, what madness! Any father is interested in the sons he has procreated (or permitted) out of the mere confusion of happiness; it was natural that the magician should fear for the future of that son whom he had thought out entrail by entrail, feature by feature, in a thousand and one secret nights. His misgivings ended abruptly, but not without certain forewarnings. First (after a long drought) a remote cloud, as light as a bird, appeared on a hill; then, toward the South, the sky took on the rose color of leopard's gums; then came clouds of smoke which rusted the metal of the nights; afterwards came the panic-stricken flight of wild animals. For what had happened many centuries before was repeating itself. The ruins of the sanctuary of the god of Fire was destroyed by fire. In a dawn without birds, the wizard saw the concentric fire licking the walls. For a moment, he thought of taking refuge in the

water, but then he understood that death was coming to crown his old age and absolve him from his labors. He walked toward the sheets of flame. They did not bite his flesh, they caressed him and flooded him without heat or combustion. With relief, with humiliation, with terror, he understood that he too was a mere appearance, dreamt by another.

your dream? This would be a dream in which the protagonist was not you but simply a dream character, as unreal or as real as all the other characters in the dream, but with the difference that the dream was narrated from her point of view, that her entire inside life would be transparent to you. This would be a situation in which 'you' are in the head of some dreamt-up John Malkovich, but without being able to access 'your' memories, beliefs, and desires (as opposed to the memories, beliefs, and desires of the dream character). If this character asks herself whether she is awake or asleep, surely the right answer is neither. She is just dreamt and would disappear as soon as her dreamer wakes up.

Could *we* be a dream character dreamt up by another? This possibility is the mirror-image of solipsism: now the suggestion is not that we are real, and everything else is not (since it is just in our mind), but rather that other things are real, and that we are not. This suggestion might well strike you as fantastic. Isn't our own existence the most basic certainty we have? And if we are just dreamt, who dreams us? God? An evil demon? Something indescribable?

Fortunately, there is a way of spelling out this 'anti-solipsism' in a way that does not require belief in God, powerful spirits, or other kinds of mysterious agents. The key lies in the notion of simulation. Simulations allow us to build extremely simple model worlds in order to test our theories, such as theories of the weather, the spread of diseases, population dynamics, the behaviour of fundamental particles, traffic jams, and much more.

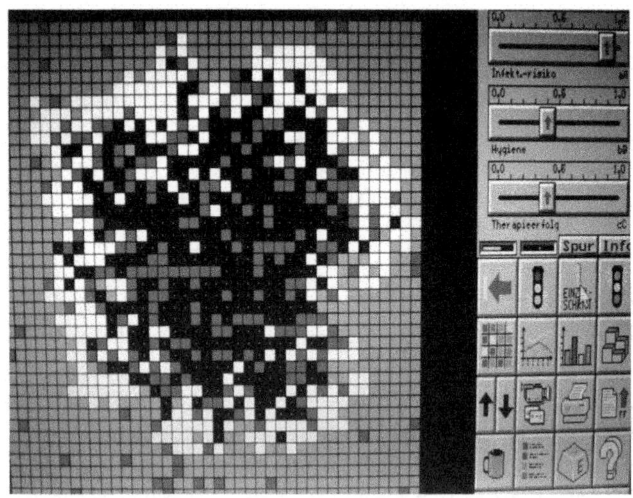


**4. Spread of an infectious disease modelled by a cellular automaton. Black cells are dead, dark grey ones infected, white ones immune. The menu on the right-hand side allows adjustment of parameters such as the infectiousness of the disease**

Usually, simulations only represent a few features of the objects they simulate and leave out most of the others. A simulation of traffic in a particular part of town intended to study what causes the traffic jams might represent the individual cars as coloured dots on the screen, for example, but it will not simulate the workings of the engines of each particular car. This is no problem, since the simulation only has to represent the aspects of the world we are interested in. Furthermore, the more detail we simulate, including molecules, atoms, and subatomic particles, the smaller the slice of the world we can represent in a simulation using present-day computing power. If our computational resources increase in the way we expect them to, or even more, these limitations may disappear in the not-too-distant future. Our vastly advanced technological descendants may be able to run simulations of physical systems as large as the planet earth, representing all details down to the atomic level.

## Simulating infectious diseases with cellular automata

To understand what a cellular automaton is, just imagine a grid of square cells, like a sheet of graph paper. Each cell is either filled in ('alive') or blank ('dead'). Assume alive and dead cells are distributed at random across the square grid. Now imagine a set of rules that determines what happens on the grid in the future. Each cell (apart from those at the corners) will have eight neighbours: two horizontal, two vertical, and four diagonal. One of our rules could say that for any cell that has more than three alive neighbours, things get a bit crowded: it dies of overpopulation. Another rule might say that cells with fewer than two alive neighbours are not happy either: they die of loneliness. We can now take our random distribution of alive and dead cells on the grid and apply the two rules to it: all cells with more than three or fewer than two neighbours are made blank, all others stay alive. We can do all of this with a sheet of graph paper, a pencil, and an eraser, but we can be much faster by getting a computer to do it. Each application of the rules is regarded as one tick of the clock in our model world. As the computer applies the rules to the grid again and again, we can see how the model world changes, causing different patterns to emerge.

What patterns emerge depends crucially on the kinds of rules that govern the transition from one state of the grid to another, and thus from one 'tick' of the clock to the next. If we want to study the spread of infectious diseases, we can postulate that some of the alive cells are ill: they carry the disease. If a healthy cell has an ill neighbour, we can have a rule that specifies the probability of it getting infected. If this is 0.5, half of the healthy cells with an ill neighbour will be ill as well after the next tick. This probability corresponds to the infectiousness of the disease – how easy it is to catch it. Another rule can specify how long an ill cell survives, that is, after how many ticks it changes from being alive to being dead. This corresponds to the virulence of the disease: how quickly it kills the cell that has it. By varying the rules, we can observe in our model world how diseases that differ in the likelihood of getting them and in the speed by which they kill develop. We will see, for example, that diseases that are very infectious and kill quickly do not spread very fast: the host will not get very far before the illness leaves him dead.

It is interesting to ask the question what we would simulate if such technology were available to us. One thing that immediately comes to mind is our own history. We often wonder how things would have worked out if small but crucial details of the past had been different. What would have happened if on 28 June 1914, the driver of Archduke Franz Ferdinand had not taken a wrong turn into a side street in Sarajevo? What if on 28 September 1928, Alexander Fleming had thrown away the contaminated Petri dish? If Mao Zedong had died of a heart attack during the famous swim in the River Yangtze on 16 July 1966? If in 1876, Alois Schicklgruber had not changed his family name to 'Hitler'? Even though we are not able to answer these questions, our descendants will. They could just run a large computer simulation of everything that happened on earth between 1875 and 1945, change one small detail in the actual course of events, and observe whether there really would have been millions of Germans shouting 'Heil Schicklgruber'. Similar simulations would allow our descendants to find out what a world without World War I would have been like, or one in which there was no penicillin, or no Cultural Revolution.

But now there is the worrying possibility that *we ourselves* exist in one of these variant simulations. Perhaps the events between 1950 and 2050 haven't actually happened the way we remember them. Perhaps one crucial detail of what really happened in 1950 (we do not know which) was changed in the simulation, and things have developed very differently since then. People with our names might not have even been born in the original run of the 1950–2050 events, in which case we are wholly the product of a simulation. Like the magician in Borges's story, we only exist in somebody else's dream.

'But this can't be right', we might think. 'We know that characters in a computer game, for example, are not conscious, but that we are. And for that reason, we can't be characters in a computer game, or for that matter, characters in a historical simulation, which is just a particularly complex computer game. There is no way the world looks like from the perspective of Lara Croft, but there is a way it looks like from our perspective. So we can't be somebody like her.' At this point, it is worthwhile to ask ourselves why we think Lara Croft is not conscious. The answer is that no computer program we have available right now is even able to simulate a good amateur Go player, let alone a wholly conscious mind in a virtual environment. If the problem is just lack of complexity, though, this is an issue that can easily be addressed. The underlying assumption was that our descendants will have access to vastly more advanced computational resources than we do, and that they will, for example, be able to simulate an entire brain, molecule by molecule. If we believe that the human mind is what the human brain does, then a simulation at that level of detail would necessarily also simulate a human mind. And part of what this means is that this mind would have a first-person perspective, that is, a way the world looks to it.

In other ways, the simulation might make shortcuts. There is no need to simulate the very small or the very far away, such as the micro-organisms in a drop of water or the rocks one metre under the surface of the moon. It is sufficient that such simulations are provided just in time, should we happen to put the drop of water under a microscope, or drill holes into the moon's surface. Similarly, computational resources might be saved by not simulating the brains of some characters in the simulation. These might appear to have the same internal structure as other people we meet, but in fact they are not much more complex than characters in contemporary computer games, virtual robots that are mere façades, giving the appearance of being conscious while in fact lacking a mind. This kind of computational cost-cutting raises the nightmare scenario in which we ourselves are not real (because we are merely simulated) and everybody else we meet is a zombie (because only their outsides are simulated).

Given that not every molecule in the world has to be simulated, but just the surfaces of most things, together with a requisite number of brains, running historical simulations of the kind described above is likely to be possible with the computational resources available in the not too distant future. Of course, it could be the case that human civilization is destroyed (hit by an asteroid, extinguished by a genetically engineered killer virus, drowned by rising sea-levels) before it can build computers powerful enough to run historical simulations. In this case, we obviously could not be living in a simulation run by our descendants. Alternatively, even if they were able to run such simulations, they might just not be interested in doing so. The insights they might gain from these might be minimal to them, and there would be other pursuits, unknown to us, that were intellectually more appealing to them. But if it is true that the computational resources required for running historical simulations won't just become available at a future time astronomically far from us, but are within our technological reach, then it seems that we don't have to make extravagant assumptions concerning the time left for us on this planet, or the changing patterns of human intellectual interests. The chance for historical simulations existing at some point in the future appears to be considerable.

Once our ancestors begin running historical simulations, the number of people existing in these simulations may quickly exceed that of the 100 billion humans who ever lived on earth. In this case, it would be rational for us to believe that it is more likely than not that we are living in a historical simulation ourselves. Suppose your friend shows you a new Dali print he just bought. Taking into account that, according to experts' opinion, 90% of such prints currently on the market are fakes, and assuming that neither you nor your friends are sufficiently well trained to distinguish an original Dali print from a fake, it would be rational for you to assume that the probability of this print being a fake is 0.9. Similarly, if n% of all conscious beings are simulated, and assuming that from your own perspective, you are not able to tell a simulation from reality, the probability of you being merely simulated is n%. (The Australian philosopher David Chalmers once estimated this probability as 20% – in the light of the above considerations, this figure seems somewhat low.)

Of course, the very same argument can be run for our descendants simulating us – they too might just be simulations of *their* descendants. In fact, if we are simulating other people, we should believe more strongly that we ourselves are simulated, since we know that such feats can be carried off. So our simulating descendants should find it even more likely that they are simulated than we do. We can imagine an entire hierarchy where we are only characters in a historical simulation run by our descendants, who are in turn simulated by others, who live in a simulation run by yet others, and so on, *ad infinitum*. In such a scenario, the simulations become more and more complicated the further down we go. The people who run the simulation two levels down in the hierarchy don't just have to simulate an entire world and all the people in it (namely our descendants), but also all the historical simulations they are running (amongst other things, us). As a simulator, one has to be careful and watch one's creation closely: if the simulated beings simulate other beings, and they create others, before we know it, all our computational resources are consumed by the simulation. The only option that may be left open to us is to switch off the simulation we are running, together with the entire hierarchy resting on it. But this might give us pause for thought. If we start running our own ancestor simulations, we raise the chance that our simulators switch us off (if we are indeed simulated), since the additional resources we use in this way may be too much. If we are at the top of a simulation-hierarchy, our simulation could be the computational straw that breaks the simulated camel's back. We should therefore think twice about running an ancestor simulation ourselves.

The simulation scenario shares some of the consequences of the other possibilities mentioned above in which we are systematically deceived: that we are dreaming, or that we are an artificially animated brain fed artificial information. We would be wrong in the majority of our beliefs, and our impulses towards virtuous behaviour might turn out to have no foundation (if we are part of a cost-cutting simulation that simulates other people as merely empty façades). But while in these two earlier cases, there is still our self, the real I that is the fixed point in the illusory vortex, in the simulation scenario we are just as unreal as the simulated world we interact with. Part of the uneasiness we feel in connection with the animated brain scenario is that the simulation might suddenly stop, and then we would realize what the real world is like: we still exist, but in radically different surroundings, at a time far in the future, without a body, in a jar, and so forth. But in the simulation case, there is no 'waking up' in the real world, since the real world, the world of our descendants, does not contain us. If the simulation stops, we won't suddenly be confronted with the fact that all our surroundings have been fake, since *we* won't exist any more. On the one hand, we might be relieved by this: we will not find ourselves to be a lone brain in an evil scientist's lab. But on the other hand, this leaves us feeling strangely insubstantial. It is no longer the case that the real world revolves around us, since we are not even part of the real world. The seemingly most fundamental certainty, that in the middle of the most intricate deceptions I, the deceived subject, still exist, has vanished. The deception could not disappear without us disappearing along with it, since we are one of the deceptions ourselves.

**5. Traditional Chinese depiction of the butterfly dream**



While the hypothesis that we do not exist at the fundamental level of reality is mind-boggling, it is possible to give the screw another turn. The fundamental idea was most famously described in the 4th century BC in an argument put forward by the Chinese philosopher Zhuangzi. He relates the following experience:

> Last night myself, Zhuangzi, dreamt he was a butterfly, a butterfly flying about, feeling that it was enjoying itself. I did not know that it was Zhuangzi. Suddenly I awoke, and was myself again, the veritable Zhuangzi. I did not know whether it had formerly been Zhuangzi dreaming that he was a butterfly, or it was now a butterfly dreaming that it was Zhuangzi. But between Zhuangzi and a butterfly there must be a difference.

In this scenario, we don't just have one person dreamt into existence by another, but two characters, Zhuangzi and the butterfly, who dream *each other* into existence. This case of symmetric dreams not only suggests that we, as a dreamt character, are not real, while somebody else, who is dreaming us, is real, but, in addition, undermines the possibility of drawing a distinction between who is real and who is not real in the first place. Zhuangzi dreams of the butterfly, so the dreamer Zhuangzi is real, and the dreamt butterfly is not. But the butterfly also dreams of Zhuangzi, who, as being dreamt, should not be real. But nothing can be both real and unreal.

Even in the simulation scenario, we could be certain that, although we were not real, somebody was. We, as simulated beings, may not be part of the most basic level of reality, but our simulators are. And if these aren't, then those who simulate them are. Somebody, in the end, is going to be real. But if we translate Zhuangzi's idea to the simulation scenario, we have a case in which we run a simulation of simulated beings, and these run a simulation of equally simulated beings in turn – and these latter simulated beings are identical with us. The simulation hierarchy has been closed up into a loop.



An interesting visual representation of such a closed loop can be seen in M. C. Escher's *Print Gallery*. It depicts a young man in a picture gallery, looking at a print with a harbour and a city behind it. As we enter the picture and examine the city, we see a woman sitting at a window above a picture gallery, in which the very same young man is looking at the picture we are currently in! As in the Zhuangzi scenario, where it is impossible to tell whether we are inside or outside of a dream, or a simulation, in this case it is impossible to determine whether the man is outside of the picture, and therefore real, or part of the picture itself, and therefore unreal. There are equally good reasons for either view: if we start with the man, we see that he stands in front of the picture, if we start with the picture, we see that the man is clearly in it. The problem is not just that we don't *know* which view is right. Neither position can be the finally correct one, since there is no additional information to be gained, no further facts we could appeal to that would settle how matters really are. After doubting

**6. M. C. Escher's *Print Gallery***



if the world around us is real, or whether we ourselves are real, it seems as if yet another certainty has gone out of the window: that no matter what the world is like, somebody or something is fundamentally real, even if we are not.

# Chapter 2
# Is matter real?

When Neo and Morpheus first meet in a simulated reality called 'the Construct', Morpheus suggests a way of defining what reality is:

> 'What is "real"? How do you define "real"? If you mean what we can taste, smell, hear and feel then what's "real" is nothing more than electrical signals interpreted by your brain.'

In other words, real is what appears to your senses. This definition, which we will call the *Matrix definition*, is curious in a number of ways. Electrons, the number 5, the latest recession – none of these are things we can taste, smell, hear, and feel, yet most people agree that they are real. On the other hand, the hallucinated insects appearing to an alcoholic during *delirium tremens*, a child's imaginary friends, and the illusory smells experienced by patients suffering from Alzheimer's disease *are* seen, heard, and smelled, yet they are not real. We need a better definition.

That something appears to our senses is not sufficient evidence for its reality. Hallucinations and related phenomena are all unreal, we say, because they cannot be seen, touched, or smelled by anyone else. They are not accessible to the senses of anyone who does not have the hallucination. We could therefore define 'real' to mean anything that appears to the senses of a sufficiently large number of observers. This will allow us to draw a line between our private imaginings and hallucinations and the appearance of a shared, public world. The mark of the real is not that it appears to some people at some time, but that it appears to most people most of the time. This idea that reality is brought about by a multitude of minds working in unison is given a sinister twist in George Orwell's *Nineteen Eighty-Four* when inner party member O'Brien notes:

> 'I tell you Winston, that reality is not external. Reality exists in the human mind, and nowhere else. Not in the individual mind, which can make mistakes, and in any case soon perishes: only in the mind of the party, which is collective and immortal.'

Let's call this the *1984 definition*. While it is more satisfactory than the Matrix definition, it is also quite weak. It will regard the flimsy façades of dystopian scenarios like *Nineteen Eighty-Four* or *The Matrix* as real, and it will also deliver strange results in less fantastic set-ups. Consider Koro, a peculiar disease found primarily in South-East Asia. Its symptoms include sudden and intense anxiety that one's genitals will recede into one's body, thereby causing death. The illness frequently occurs in Koro epidemics; a well-documented episode in Singapore in 1967 led to the admission of 97 patients into a single hospital on one day. The disease is complicated by the fact that anxious sufferers will resort to clamps, pegs, and a variety of mechanical means to stop the perceived shrinkage of their genitals inside their bodies, and these measures often cause considerable damage. Needless to say, there is no actual shrinkage to be observed. Koro is not a disease of the body, but a disease of the mind. But, according to the 1984 definition, if sufficient numbers of people *believe* in penis shrinkage, penis shrinkage is real. The difficulty with hallucinators, children with imaginary friends, and so forth, it seems, is not that they are mistaken about the way the world is, but that they are in a minority. As soon as we have enough people holding a false belief, whatever they believe in would have to be considered as real.

It would be good if we can come up with a more substantive definition of 'real' than one in terms of intersubjective agreement. The following anecdote about the lexicographer Samuel Johnson gives us an idea of what we should be looking for:

> After we came out of the church, we stood talking for some time together of Bishop Berkeley's ingenious sophistry to prove the nonexistence of matter, and that every thing in the universe is merely ideal. I observed, that though we are satisfied his doctrine is not true, it is impossible to refute it. I never shall forget the alacrity with which Johnson answered, striking his foot with mighty force against a large stone, till he rebounded from it - 'I refute it thus.'



The mark of the real, for Johnson, is the resistance certain objects put up. I can imagine a chair in front of me in all details, its shape, colours, surface, until I have the most vivid picture in my mind. Still, if I try to sit down on it, my body will land on the ground, while a real chair will keep me supported. 'Resistance', in this context, does not just mean impenetrability, but the unwillingness of real things to be influenced by our wishes and desires. As Philip K. Dick put it, a real thing is one which, when you stop believing in it, doesn't go away.

Once your child stops believing in the imaginary friend, the friend disappears. If you stop visualizing the chair, the imaginary chair will go out of existence. This is why, unlike ordinary friends and chairs, these are not real. We'll call the definition of reality as that which we don't make up *Johnson's definition*. Despite its hard-headed, common-sensical appeal, it has some strange consequences. Ordinarily, we think that the stock market is real, and dreams are not, but according to Johnson's definition, it is just the other way round. We don't make up our dreams, since we can't decide what we want to dream about (ask anyone who suffers from recurrent nightmares). And dreams put up quite a bit of resistance to our wishes and desires. If you have one of those dreams in which you are missing a train, your dream-train is not going to leave five minutes later just because you wish to catch it. It'll leave precisely on dream-time, and you are just going to miss it. The stock market, on the other hand, is something we collectively make up. If everybody stopped believing in it, that is, stopped buying and selling, the shares, their prices, and their fluctuations would just go out of existence, like an imaginary friend a child has forgotten about.

But perhaps we can fix the problem with Johnson's definition. Both dreams and the stock market are something created by human minds after all. But imagine a world in which there are no humans, or perhaps no minds whatsoever. Might we not regard all that as real that is left in such a world? What would our world be like without conscious minds? The moon would still go round the earth, and the earth round the sun; electrons would circle the nucleus of an atom. There would be no colours, but still light of different wavelengths; no scents, but still molecules suspended in air; no stories, but still marks on paper. We'll call this understanding of what is real as what is left in a world without us, a world from which all humans have been removed, the *apocalyptic definition*. While this definition lets the set of real things come out as fairly minimal (the world economy, languages, wars, amongst other things, would not be real), it is the most solid one we have met so far. It equates what is real with what is there anyway, with a world untouched by human minds, a world from which all human wishes, desires, and concerns have been taken away.



Yet it might be possible to make this definition even more solid. In his *Essay Concerning Human Understanding*, John Locke mentions an Indian who,

> saying that the world was supported by a great elephant, was asked what the elephant rested on; to which his answer was, a great

> tortoise. But being again pressed to know what gave support to the broad-backed tortoise, replied, something, he knew not what.

When we analyse the furniture of the world around us, the shoes and ships and sealing-wax we interact with every day turn out to be composed of molecules, which are in turn made up of atoms. Each atom consists of a tiny nucleus encircled by electrons. The nucleus is composed of protons and neutrons, which can be broken down into a variegated zoo of subatomic particles. All of these might be explained in terms of strings, which may in turn be reduced to a more fundamental entity, 'we know not what'. In this hierarchy, each level depends on the level directly below it, and what is real, we might want to say, is only the level others depend on, but which depends on no others, the fundamental turtle – whatever this is – grounding the entire universe. This *turtle definition* of reality differs from the apocalyptic definition because it does not regard all features of a world without minds as real: Mount Everest, for example, though mind-independent, still depends for its existence on other, smaller, more fundamental physical objects. Real is only the thing or things where the metaphysical buck stops, the objects that form the rock-bottom of the dependence chain that goes all the way from medium-sized dry goods through molecules, atoms, subatomic particles, to a destination yet unknown.



### The five definitions of reality

*Matrix definition*: Real is what appears to us.

*1984 definition*: Real is what appears to most people.

*Johnson's definition*: Real is what we don't make up.

*Apocalyptic definition*: Real is what's there anyway.

*Turtle definition*: Real is where the buck stops.

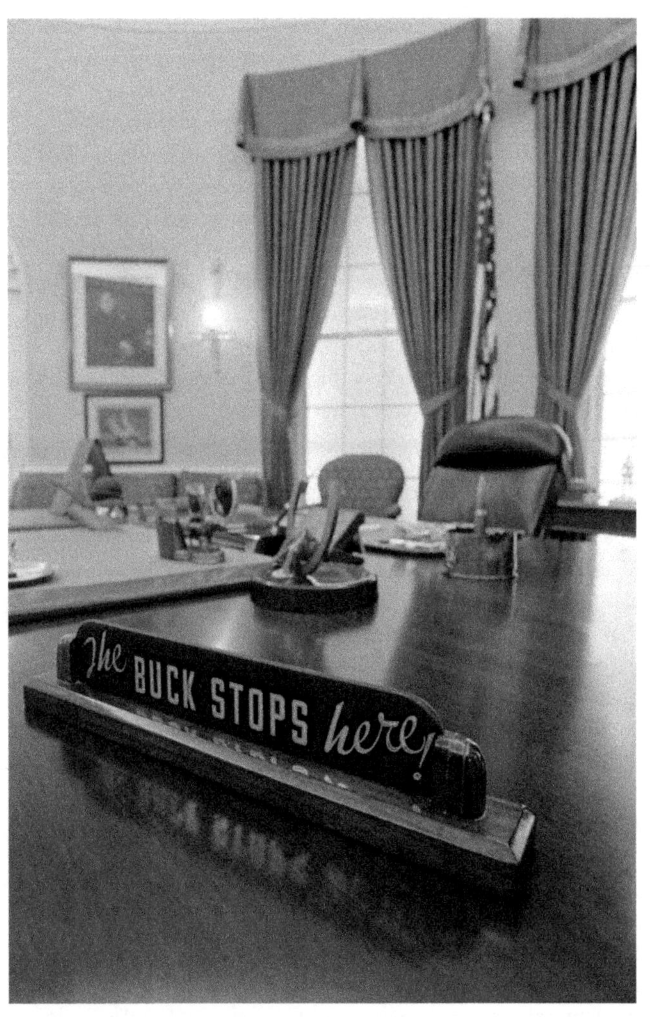


7. **Sign on Harry S. Truman's desk**

Of the five definitions of reality presented so far, the last two, defining 'real' to be what is there anyway, or what grounds everything else there is, appear to be the most solid and substantial. So when we investigate whether some kind of object is real or not, it is these two notions we should have in mind. We will start by looking at the reality of what seems to be one of the most fundamental kinds of thing: matter. A crucial question to consider is whether at the bottom level matter is like a jar of jelly or like a bucket of shot. In other words, if we take some material object and cut it in half, then cut the halves in half, and continue in this way, do we end up with simple, extended, continuous objects that, like pieces of jelly, can still be divided but have no actual parts? Or is everything made up of minute unextended atoms, like very small indivisible pieces of shot?

The jelly analogy seems to run into difficulties if we consider two objects, say, two oranges, of different sizes. Intuitively, we would want to say that one is larger than the other because it has more parts. But if matter is like jelly, there are only potential parts: we can always cut what we have in two parts again, but the world does not come pre-packaged into separate, distinct atomic parts. In this case, each orange has infinitely many potential parts. If we also assume that the internal arrangement of the two pieces of fruit is more or less the same, it is then hard to see why one orange is larger than the other.

If the world is not like jelly, are there infinitely small pieces of matter? On the face of it, this theory is much more plausible. When we cut things up, we reach some point where we cannot go on any more. The indivisible things we end up with are the fundamental, atomic constituents of matter everything is made up of. But how everything is made up of partless atoms is less straightforward than it appears. Take a complex thing consisting of three atoms, one in the middle, one each on the left and right.

**8. The Indian philosopher Vasubandhu (4th century AD)**

Call the portion where the left-hand side atom touches the middle one A, that where the middle one touches the right-hand side one B. A and B can't be the same, otherwise the left-hand side and the right-hand side atom would touch directly, and there would be only two atoms, not three. But if they are not the same, the middle atom consists of at least two portions, A and B. But how can it do so, if it has no parts? It seems that either (contrary to our assumption) atoms have to have parts, and thus are not really atoms, or a multitude of atoms cannot fill more space than a single one, in which case extended objects could not be made up of atoms.

Difficulties in spelling out what exactly matter is like along the lines just described caused the 4th-century Indian philosopher Vasubandhu to conclude that matter does not exist at all. For Vasubandhu, all that exists is mental in nature, and what we conventionally regard as matter are merely wrongly conceived mental objects. Matter is only real in the relatively weak 'Matrix' and '1984' senses of real, but not in any of the more substantial ones.

But how severe are these difficulties? Contemporary Western science has certainly embraced the 'pieces of shot' theory of matter. So how could we make sense of the atoms they postulate? We might want to respond to Vasubandhu's criticism by saying that while there are extended atoms that fill a region of space, these atoms do not have parts. We can imagine each of these atoms as surrounded by a field of a repulsive force that prevents anything from getting in. So a collection of such force-fields, each centred around an unextended atom, could fill up a volume of space, keeping any other object from occupying the space at the same time. Alternatively (and leaving the classical conception behind), we could argue that a point-particle can fill a volume by having a non-zero probability of occupying every point within that volume.

Yet it is not clear whether any of this can provide us with a plausible account of matter filling space. If we investigate any section of such a space, we notice that it is not filled: we find an unextended atom (which by definition cannot fill space) or a force-field (which is the purely negative property of not letting anything come where it is) or the *possibility* that something could be at that point. So all we end up with is the *appearance* of matter filling a region of space, without there being anything actually filling it. Whether the critic of Vasubandhu would be any happier with this option is at least debatable.

Much later, we find George Berkeley (1685–1753) also denying the reality of matter, though for reasons different from those of Vasubandhu. Berkeley points out that we never make any direct contact with matter: when we take up an orange, peel it, taste, and smell it, we become acquainted with a variety of perceptions: a round shape, a yellow-reddish colour, a sharp, perhaps sweet, citrus taste. The material object, the orange, is something we assume to exist out there as the cause of our perceptions. But we can never step outside of our own mind to check whether it is really there, independent of all perceptions. So it seems as if the idea of matter does not play a large role in our direct interactions with the world. In the end, all our theories deal with are our perceptions, and these are not material. Thus, all we are directly acquainted with is mental in nature, while the material world (if there is such a thing) is completely inaccessible. All the science we do now can be done, perhaps in a somewhat more cumbersome manner, by dispensing with talk of matter altogether, and by replacing it with talk about perceptions. Moreover, Berkeley argues, matter is not just something forever beyond our grasp, both in everyday life and in the pursuit of natural science, assuming that matter exists also does not explain anything at all. We are able to tell a long and complicated story of how the light bouncing off the orange hits our eyes, excites the photosensitive cells in our retina, which then cause impulses to travel along the optic nerve up to the brain, where they are processed in the visual cortex. But at no point does this story explain how the *perception of the orange*, which is a mental process, comes about. All that talk about matter appears to give rise to is more talk about matter, without getting anywhere close to explaining the only things we are directly acquainted with, namely our perceptions. The reality of matter is a hypothesis we can do without.

It is important to note that when Vasubandhu and Berkeley deny the reality of matter, they do not deny that it *appears* to us, or to most people. But they deny its reality in terms of the apocalyptic and the turtle definition of reality: in a world without minds, there would be no matter; furthermore, material things are not the most fundamental things there are in the world. (Vasubandhu and Berkeley also would not regard matter as real according to Johnson's definition. For them, if we all got rid of our mistaken beliefs in material objects, there would be no more matter. It is, therefore, something we collectively make up.)

Arguments like the ones put forward by Vasubandhu and Berkeley occupy an important place in the history of philosophy, yet some of the most fascinating contemporary ideas about the reality of matter do not spring from pure philosophical reflection, but from a set of relatively simple physical experiments. Attempts to explain what is going on in these experiments led to some very peculiar and often highly counterintuitive theories of the world around us.



The basic set-up of one of these experiments can easily be replicated at home. All you need is a lamp, a set of pieces of cardboard with holes in decreasing sizes, and some sort of projection screen, such as a white wall. If you put a piece of cardboard between the lamp and the wall, you see a bright patch where the light goes through the hole in the cardboard. As you replace the cardboard by pieces with smaller and smaller holes, the patch will decrease in size. Once we get beyond a certain size, however, the pattern on the wall changes from a small dot to a series of concentric dark and light rings, rather like an archery target. You can easily observe this so-called 'airy pattern' by making a very small hole (about a tenth of a millimetre) in a piece of aluminium foil and looking through this at a point-like source of light, such as a distant street lamp. The airy pattern is a characteristic sign of a wave, be it sound, water, or any other kind of wave, being forced through a hole. In itself, this is not very surprising. After all, we know that light is a wave, so it should display wave-like behaviour.

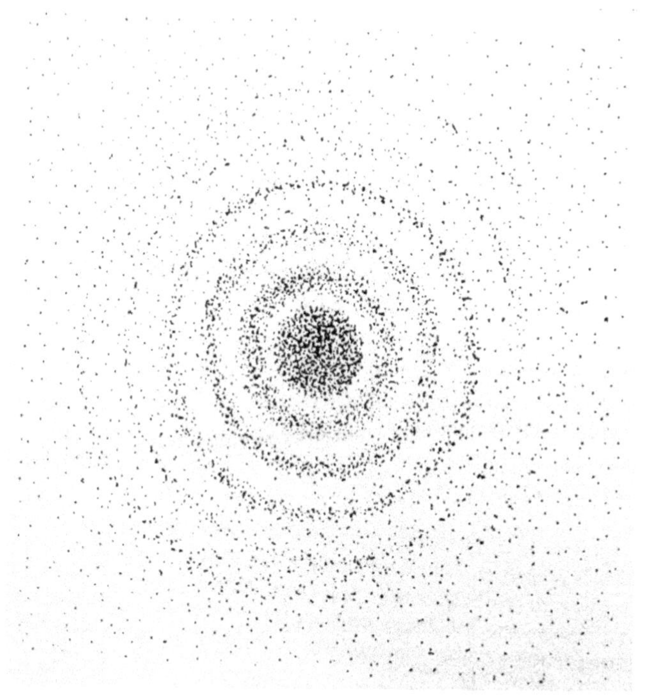

**9. Airy pattern**



But now consider what happens if we change the set-up of the experiment a bit. Instead of a lamp, we use some device shooting out electrons (such as found in old-fashioned TV sets), and instead of the wall, we use a plate of glass coated with phosphor. When an electron strikes a piece of phosphor, it lights up – we can therefore use this screen to track the places where the invisible electrons hit. The results correspond to those of the previous experiment: with sufficiently large holes, we get a more or less well-defined patch where the electrons hit the screen; with smaller holes, we get an airy pattern. This seems to be peculiar: electrons are particles located at precise points that cannot be split. Yet they seem to behave like waves that are smeared across space, are divisible, and merge into one when they meet another wave. But perhaps it is not that strange after all. Water consists of tiny particles as well, namely atoms combined into $H_2O$ molecules, yet it behaves like a wave. The emergence of the airy pattern could just be seen as something that happens when enough particles come together, whether they are water molecules or electrons. A simple variant of the above experiments shows, however, that this view cannot be right. In this variant, we reduce the number of electrons leaving our electron gun more and more, so that at the end there is only one going out every minute. The airy pattern is gone, all we see now is a small flash every minute. We now let this set-up run for some time, but keep recording where on the screen the small flash occurs. Afterwards, we map the locations of all the thousands of flashes that have occurred on the screen. Surprisingly, we do not end up with a random arrangement of dots, but with the airy pattern again! This result is extremely strange. No individual electron knows where all the earlier and later electrons are going to hit, so they cannot communicate amongst each other to produce the bull's-eye pattern. Rather, each electron must have travelled like a wave through the hole in order to produce the characteristic pattern, then changed back into a particle to produce the point-like pattern on the screen. This strange behaviour is shared by any sufficiently small piece of matter, such as electrons, neutrons, photons, quarks, or other elementary particles, but not just by these. Similar effects have been observed for objects that are large enough in principle to be seen under a microscope, such as a lattice of sixty carbon atoms shaped like a soccer ball (a so-called 'buckyball').

In order to explain their peculiar behaviour, physicists associate a *wave function* with each such object. Despite the fact that such a wave has the usual properties of more familiar waves (sound or water waves, for example), including amplitude (how far up or down it deviates from the rest state), phase (at what point in a cycle the wave currently is), and interference (so that 'up' and 'down' phases of meeting waves cancel each other out), what these new waves are waves in is not at all transparent. Einstein aptly spoke of a 'phantom field' as their medium. For a wave in an ordinary medium such as water, we can calculate its energy at any one point by taking the square of its amplitude at that point. Wave functions carry no energy, however. The square of their amplitude at a given point rather gives us the *probability* that the particle will be observed if a detector (such as the phosphor-coated screen) is placed there. Clearly, the point where an object switches from existing as a mere probability wave, with its potential existence spread out across space, to existing as an actual, spatially localized object, such as an electron hitting the phosphor screen, is of crucial importance in this account. What exactly happens when the wave function collapses, that is, when amongst the countless possibilities where the particle could be at any moment, *one* is chosen, while all the others are rejected?



First of all, we have to ask ourselves *when* this choice is made. In the example described above, it seems this happens just before the flash on the phosphor screen. At this moment, a measurement of the electron's position was made by a piece of phosphor starting to glow because it was struck by this electron, so there must have been an electron there, and not just a probability wave. But assume we cannot actually be in the lab to observe the experiment, so we point a camera at the phosphor screen and have the result sent via a satellite link right to the computer on our desktop. In this case, the light emitted from the screen has to travel to the camera recording it, and the same episode is repeated: like the electrons, light also travels as a wave and arrives as a particle (a photon, in this case). So what reason is there to believe that the collapse of the wave function, the switch from probability wave to particle, actually occurred on the phosphor screen, and not in the camera? At first, it seemed as if the phosphor screen was the measuring device, and the electron the measured. But now the measured is the screen, and the measuring device the camera. Given that any physical object transmitting the measurement we can add on to this sequence (the camera, the satellite, our computer, our eyes, our brain) is made up of particles displaying the exact same properties as the electron we are concerned with, how can we determine *any* particular step at which to place the cut between what is measured and what is doing the measuring?

This ever-expanding chain of measured phenomena and measuring devices is called the 'von Neumann chain', after the physicist and mathematician John von Neumann.

Eugene Wigner, a colleague of von Neumann's at Princeton and fellow Hungarian, made a suggestion as to where the cut could be made. As we follow the von Neumann chain upwards, the first entity we encounter that is not made up in any straightforward fashion out of pieces of matter is the consciouness of the observer who makes the measurement. We might therefore want to say that when consciousness enters the picture, the wave function collapses and the probability wave turns into a particle. This account of course implies that if we place the entire experimental set-up of electron gun, partition with a hole, and phosphor screen in a tightly closed box, the wave function will not collapse, since there is no conscious observer involved who perceives the flash of light coming from the phosphor screen. Systems with conscious observers in them can collapse the wave function; the mere presence of non-conscious measuring devices cannot.

If the consciousness of the observer did not collapse the wave function, curious consequences would follow. As we noted above, as more and more objects get sucked into the vortex of von Neumann's chain by changing from being a measuring instrument to being part of what is measured, the 'spread-out' structure of the probability wave becomes a property of these objects too. The superposed nature of the electron that seems to be at various places at once now also affects the former measuring instruments. It has been verified experimentally that objects large enough to be seen under a microscope (such as a 60-micrometre-long metal strip) and not just the unobservably small can exhibit such superposition behaviour. Of course, we can't look through a microscope and actually see the metal strip being at two places at once, as this would immediately collapse the wave function. Yet it is clear that the indeterminacy we found at the micro-level can spread to the macro-level.

If we now abstract from the observer's consciousness, he becomes nothing but a fairly intricate measuring device, a macro-level object made of matter like the phosphor screen, the camera, and so forth. Assume we put a physicist into a hermetically sealed container, big enough to be a laboratory but completely shielded from outside influences. The physicist's task is to observe whether an electron shot at the phosphor screen precisely at noon on a Monday hits the screen at the centre of the emerging airy pattern or at the periphery. He takes note of the result and continues with other experiments. On the following Monday, we open the door to the container and the physicist tells us that the electron hit the screen at the centre. Assuming that the physicist's consciousness did not collapse the wave function, he will just have been incorporated into the von Neumann chain as yet another part of the measured system (which is now no longer just the electron but everything that goes on in the box). But this system has only been measured once we open the door and ask where the electron hit the screen. Yet this would be to assume that for a week, the physicist was in a similarly superposed state, in a state of 'suspended animation' simultaneously believing that the electron hit at the centre, and that it did not. Only by our intervention the probability wave collapses, and one of the two states becomes the real one. This is a very unintuitive conclusion, since we have to assume that the physicist didn't exist like other men during the past week, and that he certainly was not able to hold beliefs like people usually do. It is extremely difficult to imagine what would be going on in such a case, as we appear to have no idea what it would be like *for us* to be in two contradictory belief states at the same time.

But things get worse. If the physicist was not able to collapse the wave function, how can we, as humans very much like him in every respect, achieve this? Does the opening of the laboratory door not mean that we are now part of the measuring device as well? Could we be in two states at once and not know it, just like the physicist in his container? Or if we are in a definite state, whose observation is responsible for this?

The apparently paradoxical features of this scenario (usually described as 'the case of Wigner's friend') are meant to support the idea of the wave function's collapsing as soon as the first consciousness enters the measurement situation. Yet if we decide to break off the chain at this point, it follows that matter cannot be regarded as real according to the apocalyptic definition. It is plausible to assume that the effects described above do not just apply to the very small (such as electrons, photons, and similar entities), but to all objects across the board – it is only that in the macroscopic case, the results are so minute that they cannot really be observed. But if consciousness is required to turn ghostly probability waves into things that are more or less like the objects we meet in everyday life, we will not be able to say that matter is what would be there anyway, whether or not human minds were around (at least if we assume that human minds are all the minds there are).

But perhaps this reasoning is a bit too quick. First of all, can't we avoid having to postulate immaterial minds by arguing that it is some feature of the *physical* process underlying human minds that cuts von Neumann's chain? In fact, the Oxford mathematician Roger Penrose has proposed a way in which an object's wave function could collapse on its own accord without interacting with a measuring device. The fundamental idea is that systems larger than a certain critical mass collapse under their own weight, so to speak, turning one of the superposed mere possibilities into an actuality. Penrose speculates that this 'objective reduction' takes place in specific parts of the neurons

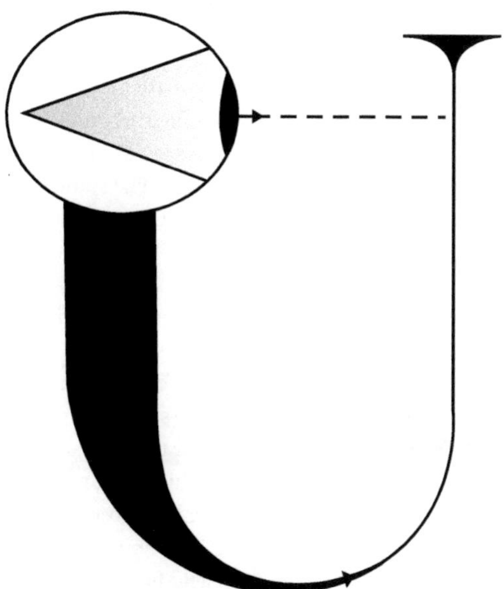

**10. Illustration of John Wheeler's participatory universe: the observer's observation creates the universe of which he is a part**



that make up the brain (so-called microtubules). If this was the case, we would not need some mysterious, non-material substance to turn a probability wave into a particle; an ordinary physical process inside our brains would be sufficient.

The conscious mind would then be the result, rather than the cause, of these quantum-level processes. Such processes, Penrose claims, endow the mind with a power beyond those of an ordinary computer, which entails that it would never be possible to build a machine functioning like the computers we know that could run a human-like mind as a program. Fascinating as these ideas are, they are also highly speculative. Neither the concept of 'objective reduction', nor the idea that this takes place within microtubules, has yet found widespread acceptance.

Second, even if we agree with the above idea that some non-material consciousness is required to break the chain, all that follows is that the dynamic attributes of matter (such as position, momentum, and spin orientation) are mind-dependent. But it does not follow that its static attributes (such as mass, charge, and spin magnitude) are dependent in this way. The static attributes are there whether we look or not, and can therefore be regarded as real in the apocalyptic sense.

We have to ask ourselves, however, whether the redefinition of 'matter' as 'a set of static attributes' preserves enough of its content to allow us to regard matter as real. In a world without minds, there would still be attributes such as mass and charge, but things would not be at any particular location or travel in any particular direction. Such a world has virtually nothing in common with the world as it appears to us. Werner Heisenberg observed that:



> the ontology of materialism rested upon the illusion that the kind of existence, the direct 'actuality' of the world around us, can be extrapolated into the atomic range. This extrapolation, however, is impossible. [...] Atoms are not things.

It seems that the best we are going to get at this point is the claim that some things are apocalyptically real, even though they have very little to do with our ordinary understanding of matter.

How real does matter turn out to be if we understand 'real' not in terms of the apocalyptic definition but in terms of the final turtle definition, taking real to be that which provides the foundation for everything else? In order to answer this question, we have to have a look at a key scientific notion, that of a reductive explanation. Much of the power of scientific theories derives from the insight that we can use one theory, applicable to a certain set of objects, to explain facts about a quite different set of objects. We therefore don't need a separate set of laws and principles to explain the second set of objects, but we can assume that all their behaviour can be reduced to statements about the first kind of objects, which can then be explained by a theory dealing with these. A good example is the way in which theories from physics and chemistry, dealing with inanimate matter, can be used in explaining processes animate objects (biological organisms) are involved in.

There is no need to postulate a special physics or a special chemistry to explain an organism's metabolism, how it procreates, how its genetic information is passed on, how it ages and dies. The behaviour of the living cells that make up the organism can be accounted for in terms of the nucleus, mitochondria, and other subcellular entities, which can in turn be explained in terms of chemical reactions based on the behaviour of molecules and the atoms that compose them. For this reason, the explanations of biological processes can be said to be reducible to chemical and ultimately to physical ones.



If we pursue the aim of a reductive explanation of the phenomena around us, a first step is to reduce statements about the medium-sized goods that surround us, about bricks, brains, bees, bills, and bacteria, to statements about fundamental material objects, such as molecules. We then realize everything about these can be explained in terms of their constituents, namely the atoms. Atoms, of course, have parts as well, and we are now well on our way through the fascinating realm of smaller and smaller subatomic particles. No most fundamental objects have been reached so far; in fact, there is not even an agreement that there are any such objects. Yet this is no reason to stop our explanations here, since we can always understand the most basic physical objects in terms of the parts of space and time they occupy. So instead of having our explanation talk about a certain particle that exists at such-and-such a place for such-and-such a period of time, we can simply reduce this to talk about a certain spatial region with specific coordinates that is occupied between two different times.

Yet we can go even more fundamental. If we take an arbitrary fixed point in space, and a stable unit of spatial distance, we can determine any other point in space by three coordinates. These simply tell us to go so many units up or down, so many units left or right, and so many units back or forth. We can do the same with points in time, determining each point in time as so many temporal units before or after a fixed temporal point. We now have a way of expressing space-time points as sets of four positive or negative numbers, x, y, z, and t, where x, y, and z represent the three spatial dimensions and t the temporal dimension. Mathematicians have found a way of reducing numbers to something yet more fundamental: sets. To do this, they replace the number 0 with the empty set (the set with nothing in it), the number 1 with the set that contains just the empty set, the number 2 with the set that contains just the set that contains just the empty set, and so on. One can then show that all the properties of numbers also hold for all these ersatz numbers made from sets.



It seems as if we have now reduced all of the material world around us to a complicated array of sets. For this reason, it is important to know what these mathematical objects called 'sets' really are. There are two views of mathematical objects that are important in this context. First, there is the view of them as Platonic objects. This means that mathematical objects are unlike all other objects we encounter. They are not made of matter, they do not exist in space or time, do not change, cannot be created or destroyed, and could not have failed to exist. According to the Platonic understanding, mathematical objects exist in a 'third realm', a world distinct from the world of matter, on the one hand, and the world of mental entities, such as perceptions, thoughts, and feelings, on the other.

Second, we have the understanding of mathematical objects as fundamentally mental in nature. They are of the same kind as the other things that pass through our mind: thoughts and plans and concepts and ideas. Yet they are not wholly subjective; other people can have the very same mathematical object in their minds as we have in ours, so that when we both talk about the Pythagorean theorem, we are talking about the same thing. But mathematical objects do not have any existence over and above the minds in which they occur.

On either of these understandings we end up with a curious result. If the bottom level of the world are sets, and if sets are not material, but rather some Platonic, alien entities, material objects have completely disappeared from view and cannot be real according to the turtle definition. If we follow scientific reduction all the way down, we end up with stuff that certainly does not look like tiny pebbles or billiard balls, not even like strings vibrating in a multidimensional space, but more like what pure mathematics deals with.

This idea is spelled out in considerable detail in the theory that the material world itself is the output of some giant computer. One set of arguments for this is based on the idea that while the behaviour of particles at the quantum level is very hard to make sense of in terms of medium-sized dry goods such as marbles and billiard balls, understanding them as the output of some program is in many ways easier.

The various objects quantum mechanics studies are indistinguishable from each other; each electron is exactly like every other electron whether it is one of the two electrons in a helium atom, or one of the seventy-nine in a gold atom. Such likeness does not usually occur in our everyday world. Leibniz famously challenged his audience in the gardens of Princess Sophie Charlotte to find any two leaves that are exactly identical. The feat could not be done. Yet if you type the name 'Leibniz' on your computer, there will be two 'i's there exactly alike each other, whether they occur between an 'e' and a 'b' or an 'n' and a 'z'. This is because all 'i's are produced by the same procedure within the computer's program. Electrons and other things like them, one could therefore argue, might be made in the same way by the computer whose computations bring about the world.

Another puzzling fact is that while the formalism of quantum mechanics associates a wave function with every object, these waves are different from ordinary waves, as there is no medium they wave in. Waves in water or air can be understood in terms of the temporary displacement of parts of their medium (i.e. the water and air molecules). For the waves quantum mechanics talks about, this interpretation is not available, as there are no more fundamental, underlying objects to show wavelike behaviour. But if we understand a wave as something encoded in a computer's memory, that is, as a sequence of 0s and 1s, there is no necessity to assume that this can only be transmitted by something that waves.

Sound-'waves' generated by a computer, for example, do not require a waving medium, since they only exist in the computer's memory. But this does not keep them from functioning just as well as any other sound waves we are familiar with.

The view that the material world is the result of an enormous computation brings us back to the idea of the universe as a computer simulation, this time not by the route of historical simulations, but as an attempt to make sense of the behaviour of the world in very small areas during very small periods of time. The underlying idea is that even though we can never see the way a computer is programmed (because the code, as a piece of abstract information, is not a physical thing), we can still, by close inspection of details of the program it is running, deduce the way it is programmed. The world of material objects we see around us, together with the space and time in which they seem to be placed, is nothing but the output of this program. They do not exist at the level of the computer's code, in the same way in which there is not one arrow-shaped thing somewhere deep in the centre of your computer that corresponds to the pointer of your mouse.

Even though a computer program can present itself to us in a variety of physical manifestations, such as text on a screen, a printout, or as stored on a computer's hard drive, it is itself not a material thing but an abstract object, something that exists necessarily, is unmade, unchangeable, and outside of space and time. If the world of matter we perceive was the result of the running of such a program, then material objects form no part of the fundamental nature of reality according to the turtle definition. If we go all the way down, we realize that the material world does not consist of minute material things, but of a peculiar type of mathematical objects.

Of course, the Platonistic view of mathematical objects is hardly uncontroversial, and many people find it hard to get any clear idea of how objects could exist outside of space and time, how we could have any knowledge of them, and how they could bring about things that do have spatial and temporal locations. But if we take mathematical objects to be mental in nature, we end up with a scenario that is even stranger than the one the Platonist imagines. For the scientific reductionist sets out to reduce the human mind to the activity of the human brain, then reduce the brain to an assembly of interacting cells, the cells to molecules, the molecules to atoms, the atoms to subatomic particles, the subatomic particles to collections of space-time points, the collections of space-time points to sets of numbers, and the sets of numbers to pure sets. But at the very end of this reduction, we now seem to loop right back to where we came from: to the mental entities.

A closely related loop results for any attempt to unify psychology, biology, and physics if we assume that consciousness plays a role in the reduction of the wave function. For this, we would try to reduce the human mind to the activity of the central nervous system, which is a biological structure. Biological structures can be accounted for in terms of chemical processes, the interaction of carbon, nitrogen, oxygen, and so forth, which can be broken down into yet smaller constituents until we reach the level where quantum phenomena become experimentally relevant. And in order to explain these, it appears, we have to bring in a phenomenon from the very top of the chain, namely the human mind.

In both cases, what we thought we should take to be the most fundamental turns out to involve essentially what we regarded as the least fundamental. In our search for foundations, we have gone round in a circle, from the mind, via various components of matter, back to the mind. But this just means that *nothing* is fundamental, in the same way as there is no first or last stop on London's Circle line. The moral to draw from the reductionist scenario described above seems to be that either what is fundamental is not material, or that nothing at all is fundamental.

We also encounter a similar curious loop in the most influential way of understanding quantum mechanics, different from the one described above, the so-called 'Copenhagen interpretation' (named after the city where the institute of its chief expositor, Niels Bohr, was based). Unlike Wigner's consciousness-based interpretation, this does not assume that the collapse of the wave function occurs when a conscious mind observes the outcome of some experiment, but already when the system to be measured (the electron in our example) interacts with the measuring device (the phosphor screen). For this reason, it has to be assumed that the phosphor screen will behave classically, and will not itself exhibit the peculiar quantum behaviour shown by the electron.

For the Copenhagen interpretation, things and processes describable in terms of familiar classical concepts are the foundation of any physical interpretation. And this is where the circularity comes in. We analyse the everyday world of shoes, ships, and sealing-wax (which includes phosphor screens, cameras, computers, our eyes, and all other medium-sized material things) in terms of smaller and smaller constituents; molecules, atoms, and subatomic particles, until we deal with parts that are so small that quantum effects become relevant for describing them. But when it comes to spelling out what our theories of quantum effects really *mean*, we don't ground them in some yet more minute micro-level structures. As Bohr himself pointed out, 'there is no quantum world. There is only a quantum physical description.' What this means is that instead of going further down, we instead jump right back up to the level of concrete phenomena of sensory perception, namely macrophysical measuring devices, such as phosphor screens and cameras, claiming that our theory is about the readings these instruments make. Once more, we are in a situation where we cannot say that the microphysical world of quantum objects is fundamental (since talk about these is just a conceptual bridge allowing us to connect certain statements about what happens to ordinary-sized measuring devices), nor can we say that the macrophysical world of measuring devices is fundamental (since these devices are themselves nothing but large conglomerations of quantum objects). We therefore have a circle of things depending on each other, even though, unlike in the previous case, mental objects are no longer part of this circle. As a result, neither the medium-sized phosphor screen nor the minute electron can be regarded as real according to the turtle definition, since neither constitutes a class of objects such that every thing depends on them, even though they depend on none.

# Chapter 3
# Are persons real?

In the spring of 1982, an American woman was waiting for a bus on the Parisian Avenue de la Grande Armée. Getting into the bus, she felt her mind exploding, and

> what I had previously called 'me' was forcefully pushed out of its usual location inside me into a new location that was approximately a foot behind and to the left of my head. 'I' was now behind my body looking out at the world without using the body's eyes.

This unsettling experience of her displaced I became even more disturbing when several days later it disappeared completely. As a result,

> the personal self was gone, yet here was a body and a mind that still existed empty of anyone who occupied them. [...] The mind, body and emotions no longer referred to anyone – there was no one who thought, no one who felt, no one who perceived. Yet the mind, body, and emotions continued to function unimpaired; apparently they did not need an 'I' to keep doing what they always did. [...] The oddest moments occurred when any reference was made to my name. If I had to write a check or sign a letter, I would stare at the letters on the paper and the mind would drown in perplexity. The name referred to no one.

The next fourteen years of her life (before dying of a brain tumour at the age of 42) were spent without her ever regaining the sense of a personal self.

This case is not unique. In 1880, the French neurologist Jules Cotard first described a rare neuropsychiatric disorder – now known as Cotard's syndrome – which in its milder forms leads the patient to assume that they are already dead or to deny the existence of their own body. In more severe developments, the sufferers may deny their very existence, often dispensing altogether with the use of the word 'I'.

Such psychological conditions are very hard for us to understand. There seem to be few things more close to home than the existence of ourselves as a person. We might be thoroughly sceptical about the existence of the world around us, wondering whether the tree in the quad and the gardener mowing the lawn really exist, but how could we be sceptical about the existence of *us*? Isn't our scepticism made impossible by the fact that there is somebody who is sceptical about something? Who, if not us, would this somebody be?



Persons are certainly real according to the Matrix definition. A person, our self, certainly appears to us, and in fact it appears to us to a greater extent and with greater persistence than anything else. A teacup that we use daily for ten minutes over five years will only be perceived by us for a total of about 300 hours. But we perceive ourselves during the whole of our waking life. In fact, our self-perception even continues during our dreams. Even though we might be wrong about most things we believe when dreaming, we can't be wrong that it's us (rather than somebody else) having this dream.

Not only do we perceive ourselves as persons, but most other people (apart from some in special psychological conditions such as those just described) perceive themselves in this way as well. Persons are therefore real according to the 1984 definition. Moreover, it appears as if we cannot just decide what person we want to be. Even though we have a limited influence on shaping our own selves, it seems that in the end much of the body, the genes, the beliefs, memories, and psychological tendencies we regard as constituting *us* are beyond our control. As our selves do not appear to be something we can just make up, they are real according to Johnson's definition too.

We saw earlier that the most substantial definitions of 'real' were the apocalyptic and the turtle definition. Persons clearly cannot be real according to the apocalyptic definition, since they would not be features of the world without us. It is hard to make sense of a world in which persons or selves exist, even though we don't. But it is much more plausible to regard persons as real according to the turtle definition. Persons, it seems, constitute an irreducible part of the world as we know it. At the fundamental level, there are not just pieces of matter, but also systems that provide a perspective on the pieces of matter, systems with a point of view. So far, we have not succeeded in reducing them to something more fundamental, and if they are not reducible in this way, they must constitute a piece of the furniture of the world at the foundational level. Persons therefore may be real in one of the most important senses of the word.

Things get a lot more puzzling, however, once we try to get a better grip of what being a person and having a self actually amount to. There seem to be four main factors involved. First of all, our self is *inside* our body, yet is distinct from it. It owns the body that supports its existence. Second, we regard ourselves as *unchanging* and continuous. This is not to say that we remain forever the same, and never change our desires, inclinations, or fundamental outlook on the world. Yet among all this change, there is something that remains constant and that makes me now the same 'me' as me five years ago and five years in the future. Third, the self is the *unifier* that brings it all together. The world presents itself to us as a disconcertingly diverse cacophony of sights, sounds, smells, mental images, recollections, deliberations, and so forth. In the self, these are all integrated and an image of a single, unified world emerges. Finally, the self is an *agent*. It is the thinker of our thoughts and the doer of our deeds. It is where the representation of the world unified into one coherent whole is used in order to act on this very world.

All of these observations appear to be blindingly obvious and as certain as anything could be. We just have to look at ourselves to see that we are not a body but something that has a body, that we move through time as more or less the same person, and that we are the central control room where data from the world get in, and from where decisions to act are sent out. But as we look at these four factors in more detail, they become less and less obvious.

We are not just the same thing as our body at any given time. Cells in our body are replaced by the normal process of metabolic turnover, and even though this replacement goes on with different speeds depending on the type of cell concerned, after a sufficiently large amount of time, each cell will have been replaced by a new one. Yet we still think we have the same self through the whole of our life. But if the self is distinct from our body, where in the body is it located? Different cultures put it in different places: the Egyptians and Aristotle preferred the heart; Homer placed the *thymos* (θυμός), the source of emotions, in the lungs; the Ancient Chinese regarded a place in the abdomen called *dantian* (丹田) as essential; and Plato, Galen, and many others chose the head or, more specifically, the brain. Of course, these can't all be right, unless we assume that the self is spread out across our entire body, and is present in all these places at once. This might strike us as the most plausible view, given the fact that if I burn my fingers, I feel a pain in myself and at the same time feel a pain in the hand. Yet this spread-out view implies that if we lose a hand or an arm, our self (not just our body) is missing a part and is now smaller than before – surely a curious consequence.

At present, the majority of people feel most comfortable with locating themselves at a spot in their head, just behind the eyes,

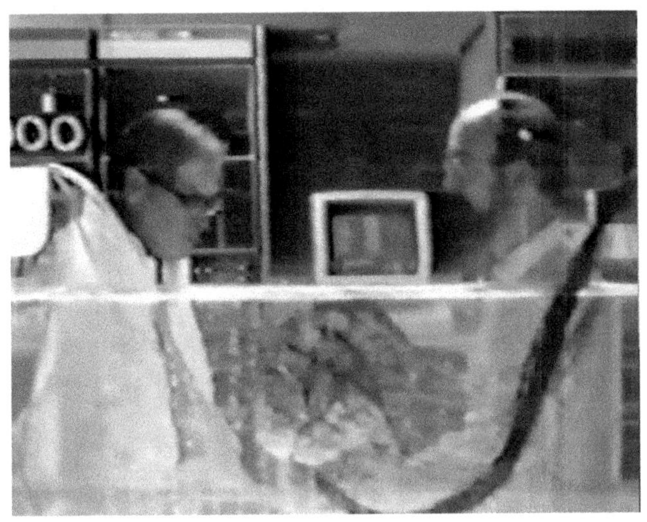

**11. Still from the film *Where Am I?*, featuring Daniel Dennett (Daniel Dennett, right) and Dennett's Brain**



looking out into the world. Some bizarre consequences of this view have been explored by the philosopher Daniel Dennett in a short story called *Where Am I?*. In the story, Dennett's brain is removed, placed in a life-support system, and each nerve connection is replaced by a pair of miniature radio transceivers, one attached to the brain, the other to the nerve-ending in Dennett's empty skull. In this way, the connection between Dennett's body and his brain has become infinitely elastic. Instead of having limited wiggle room in the cranium, constrained by the elasticity of the nerves, the brain can now be at a considerable distance from the body, while all connectivity and functionality is preserved. Problems arise when the empty-headed Dennett goes to see his own brain, for he is unable to keep up the belief that *he* is located somewhere in the brain. He keeps thinking that he is looking at his brain in a tank, though what is really happening (he should think) is that Dennett is in the tank, being looked at by his own body.

## Excerpt from Dennett's *Where Am I?*

'I gather the operation was a success,' I said. 'I want to go see my brain.' They led me (I was a bit dizzy and unsteady) down a long corridor and into the life-support lab. A cheer went up from the assembled support team, and I responded with what I hoped was a jaunty salute. Still feeling lightheaded, I was helped over to the life-support vat. I peered through the glass. There, floating in what looked like ginger ale, was undeniably a human brain, though it was almost covered with printed circuit chips, plastic tubules, electrodes, and other paraphernalia. 'Is that mine?' I asked. 'Hit the output transmitter switch there on the side of the vat and see for yourself,' the project director replied. I moved the switch to OFF, and immediately slumped, groggy and nauseated, into the arms of the technicians, one of whom kindly restored the switch to its ON position. While I recovered my equilibrium and composure, I thought to myself: 'Well, here I am sitting on a folding chair, staring through a piece of plate glass at my own brain ... But wait,' I said to myself, 'shouldn't I have thought, 'Here I am, suspended in a bubbling fluid, being stared at by my own eyes'?' I tried to think this latter thought. I tried to project it into the tank, offering it hopefully to my brain, but I failed to carry off the exercise with any conviction. I tried again. 'Here am I, Daniel Dennett, suspended in a bubbling fluid, being stared at by my own eyes.' No, it just didn't work. Most puzzling and confusing. Being a philosopher of firm physicalist conviction, I believed unswervingly that the tokening of my thoughts was occurring somewhere in my brain: yet, when I thought 'Here I am,' where the thought occurred to me was here, outside the vat, where I, Dennett, was standing staring at my brain.



But we do not have to use science-fiction scenarios like this one to see that there is something worrying about our natural belief that we, our selves, are inside our bodies. It seems to us that we inhabit our body, we feel a sense of ownership towards it. We do so in a sense that is far more substantial than a sense of ownership we could feel to a house we live in. We can live without the house, but whether we could live without our body is at least questionable, as it supports and sustains the mind that regards itself as its inhabitant. Our self, it appears, is whatever inhabits the body that sustains the functions of the mind.

Yet the kind of ownership we feel towards our body can be generated with respect to things that are not our body, things that are not alive, and even towards things that do not exist at all.

The rubber hand illusion is a particularly simple case where an inanimate object, a piece of rubber, is suddenly regarded as part of the body, and feelings are experienced in it, even though no biological processes take place in this artificial hand. Using some more advanced technology, we can produce even more



### The rubber hand illusion

To replicate the rubber hand illusion at home, you will need a rubber hand, a piece of cardboard, and two paintbrushes. If you find it difficult to get hold of a rubber hand (there is an inexpensive kind made for training manicurists), an inflated latex glove will do the trick. Put it on a table in front of you and (assuming you are using a left-handed rubber hand) put your left hand to the left of it. Put up the piece of cardboard in such a way that it forms a screen, so that you can only see the rubber hand but not your real left hand. Now get an assistant to stroke your real and your rubber hand with the two brushes at the same places at the same time. After about two minutes, you are likely to experience the peculiar sensation of feeling strokes in the rubber hand. You might even feel the presence of a 'virtual arm', that is, something connecting the rubber hand to your body.

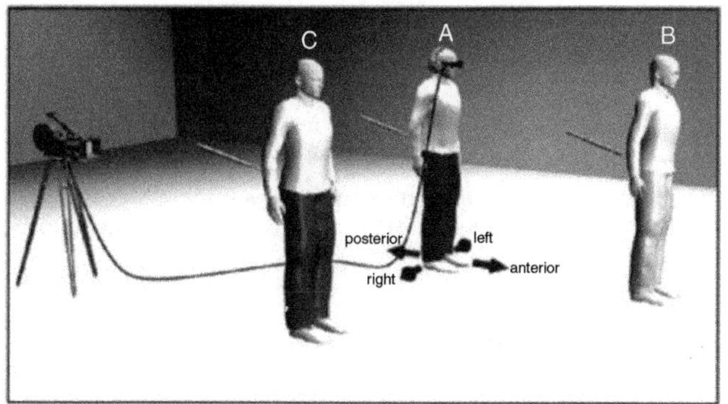


**12. Virtual full-body illusion**

peculiar effects. In an interesting experiment, the participant (A) wears a head-mounted display, consisting of a pair of special glasses that project a separate image into each eye, thereby giving the impression of being in a three-dimensional environment. The visual data projected into the participant's eyes come from a camera positioned behind his back. Looking through the head-mounted display, the subject therefore has the strange sensation of looking at his own back, standing at some distance in front of him (B) – just as in Magritte's famous painting.



If we now have someone stroke his back, that is, if the subject has the sensation of having his back stroked while seeing the back of the virtual character in front of him being stroked, he will frequently report the feeling that the virtual character was his own body; he identifies with it and attempts to 'jump into it'.

This illusion also works if we direct the camera at a mannequin (C) instead of our own body. We seem to have here a full-body equivalent of the rubber hand illusion and a particularly striking case of locating our self outside of our body. Interestingly enough, we don't locate ourselves at the centre of projection of our visual perspective (that is, at the place of the camera) but at the place of the perceived bodily image in front of us.

While it is peculiar to feel sensations in a rubber hand that does not contain any nerves, it is even stranger to do so in a hand that is not there at all. This happens to amputees suffering from a phantom limb. Not only do they feel the missing limb still to be there, they also often have the impression that their non-existent limb is twisted in a painful position and cannot be moved any more, causing great distress to the patient. The existence of phantom limbs causes difficulties for the view that our self is spread out throughout our body, and located everywhere where we can feel something. For it now seems as if the self can somehow leak out of our body and feel something where there is no body present.



If we can feel bodies made of inanimate material, or experience sensations in body parts that no longer exist, it becomes clear that the view of us existing somewhere inside our body is far from unproblematic. There is no logical or psychological necessity (and, if the scenario from Dennett's story should ever become reality, no practical necessity) forcing us to locate our self at the same place as the body that supports the existence of our mental life. Rather, it seems as if we ourselves create a cognitive model, a simulation, of a body in which we locate our self. This model can incorporate parts of inanimate matter, such as the rubber hand, as well as non-existent phenomena, such as limbs that are no longer part of our body. The location of the self is not something we find out there in the world, but something that is to a significant extent made by ourselves.

The question 'Where am I?' causes a variety of perplexing problems, and unfortunately the question 'When am I?' does not fare much better. An immediately obvious answer would be to say that we exist continuously from our first conscious moments in our mother's womb up to our death (and perhaps thereafter, if one believes in an afterlife). Yet during the eighty or so years our continuous self exists, it undergoes some quite substantial changes: bodily changes, but also changes in beliefs, abilities, desires, and moods. The happy self of today cannot be the same as the sad self of yesterday, since nothing can be at the same time happy and sad. But we surely have the same self today that we had yesterday.

We can address this problem by assuming that our self is something more fundamental, something constant that has all these changing properties but remains itself what it is. Like a thread running through every single one of a string of pearls, our self runs through every single moment of our lives, providing a core and a unity for them. The difficulty with this view of the self is that it cannot have most of the properties we usually think make me *me*. Being happy or sad, being able to speak Chinese, preferring cherries to strawberries, even being conscious – all these are changeable states the disappearance of which should not affect the self, as a disappearance of individual pearls should not affect the thread. But it then becomes unclear why such a minimal self should have the central status in our lives we usually accord to our self. If practically everything that is going on in our mental lives leaves the self untouched, what is the use of such a self?

To put the point in a different way, suppose someone offered you a drug that completely destroyed your self while leaving all your beliefs, desires, preferences, and so on intact. Would there be anything wrong with taking it? It would certainly be preferable to a drug that destroyed all our beliefs, desires, preferences, etc. and left our self intact. This might give rise to the suspicion that the self understood in this way is not what we care about, but the content of our mental lives is. Furthermore, given that you cannot tell the difference between having taken the drug and not having taken the drug from the inside, could it be the case that you have secretly been given the drug and so don't have any self any more? Should you worry about this? It would not be the case that as a pharmaceutically caused selfless creature you are lacking any experience you had before – unless there was some specific 'being me' experience completely divorced from what is going on in our mind that continued unchanged through your waking life, through sleep and deep coma. But there is no such experience. The Scottish philosopher David Hume made this point very clearly:

> For my part, if I enter most intimately into what I call myself I always stumble on some particular perception or other, of heat or cold, light or shade, of love or hatred, pain or pleasure. I never can catch myself at any time without a perception, and never can observe any thing but the perceptions.

But perhaps talk of a self does not imply that there has to be some constant thing running through our entire life like a thread in a string of pearls. A piece of rope holds together even though there is no single long fibre running through the entire rope, there is just a sequence of overlapping shorter fibres. Similarly, our self might just be the continuity of overlapping mental events. While this view has a certain plausibility, it also means that we are never wholly present. We usually assume that when we think of something or make a decision, it is the whole of us doing this, not just some specific part. Yet, according to the rope view, our self is never completely present at any point, just like a rope stretched across a ruler is not wholly present at any of the points marked on the ruler. While this is also true of the string of pearls model (since the thread is not wholly present in any pearl), at least if you put all the instances of your life together, there is some part of this whole that constitutes your self. But in the case of the rope model, no such thing exists.

It appears as if we are left with the unattractive choice between a continuous self so far removed from everything constituting us that its absence would scarcely be noticeable, and a self that did actually consist of components of our mental life, but contains no constant part that we could identify with.

There is one feature of the self that is much more important than the two we have discussed so far. This is the fact that the self is the centre of our world. It is here that it all comes together. It is easy to overlook the significance of this fact, but if we consider the task the brain has to accomplish in bringing about the appearance of a unified world, it becomes evident that it is extremely complex. The different information coming in from our senses, visual, auditory, tactile, olfactory, and gustatory sensations are processed at different regions in the brain. They have to travel different distances (a tickle at our foot has to travel further to reach the brain than a tickle at our chest) and arrive at the brain at different times. The processing speed for different kinds of sensory information varies; visual stimuli take longer to process than other stimuli. (The difference is about 40 milliseconds. To compare: speaking a single syllable takes about 200 milliseconds.) On the other hand, light travels much faster than sound. Putting together these different speeds means that sights and sound from about ten metres away are available to consciousness at about the same time; for everything closer or further away information about its sight and sound arrives at different times. In these cases, the apparent simultaneity of, for example, hearing a voice and seeing the speaker's lips move has to be constructed by our brain.

In addition, incoming sensory information has to be screened for relevance very quickly (the roar of the tiger behind us has to be attended to more quickly than the chirping of the bird in front of us). At the same time, thoughts and memories have to be processed. Yet a coherent, unified world emerges from this mess of data almost all of the time. (This only seems to break down consistently in the case of certain psychiatric disorders or when using hallucinogenic drugs.)

René Descartes stressed that such unification was necessary for a self (or soul) to gain knowledge of the world. Speaking about the pineal gland, a small body shaped like a pine cone near the centre of the brain, he remarks:

> My view is that this gland is the principal seat of the soul, and the place in which all our thoughts are formed. The reason I believe this is that I cannot find any part of the brain, except this, which is not double. Since we see only one thing with two eyes, and hear only one voice with two ears, and in short have never more than one thought at a time, it must necessarily be the case that the impressions which enter by the two eyes or by the two ears, and so on, unite with each other in some part of the body before being considered by the soul. Now it is impossible to find any such place in the whole head except this gland.

This picture of the mind is sometimes described as the 'Cartesian theatre'. Like a spectator seated in front of the stage, the self perceives the appearance of the world put together from a diverse range of sensory data. It would get confused if these had not been unified before, just as a theatregoer would be if suddenly two actors appeared on stage, each claiming to be Hamlet. While this picture is extremely natural and persuasive, it faces so many difficulties that we should be wary of being convinced by it. Consider a very simple case.

If we project a bright spot in the lower left-hand corner of a screen, followed immediately by one in the upper right-hand corner, it appears to us as if there was a single dot moving in a left–right diagonal across the screen. (This so-called beta phenomenon was discovered by psychologists early in the 20th century.) If we let the spots have different colours, for example by making the lower left spot red and the upper right spot green, we observe a single moving spot changing colour when it reaches the mid-point of the diagonal. This is a very peculiar result. If our brain fills in the missing positions along the diagonal for the benefit of the self in the Cartesian theatre, how does it know that the colour of the spot has to switch from red to green halfway along the diagonal, that is, *before* the green spot has been observed? Precognitive abilities that would allow us to know what is going to happen before it actually does are somewhat unlikely. Another way of explaining the beta phenomenon is by assuming that all our experience is played in the Cartesian theatre with a small time delay. The brain does not pass on the information about the red spot as soon as it can, but holds it back for a little while. Once the green spot has been processed, both spots are put together into a perceptual narrative that involves one moving spot changing colour. This edited version is then screened in the theatre of consciousness.

Unfortunately, this time delay explanation does not fit in well with our evidence of how perception works. Even though they are not as quick as reflexes, we know that conscious responses can occur at a speed very close to the minimal times physically possible. Once we add up how long it takes for information to travel to the brain and the response preparation time, there is not enough time left for the kind of time delay that would explain the beta phenomenon.



At this point, it makes sense to suspect that there is something wrong with the notion of a self perceiving a unified stream of sensory information. Perhaps there are just the various neurological processes taking place in the brain and the various mental processes taking place in our mind, without some central agency where it all comes together at a particular moment, the perceptual 'now'. The self we place at the focus of our mental life might just be a convenient fiction without a significant basis in fact. And if there is no specific time when a perceptual content appears in the theatre of the self (because there is no such theatre), it is much easier to make sense of the beta phenomenon. The mistaken perception of a red spot turning green arises in the brain only *after* the perception of the green spot, yet the subjectively experienced sequence can be 'red spot – red spot turning green – green spot'. When you read the sentence 'The man ran out of the house, before that he had kissed his wife', the sequence in which the information comes in is 'running – kissing', but the sequence of events you construct from this is 'kissing – running'. Since there is no objective fact about when something becomes subjectively conscious (by entering the theatre), there is no need to postulate a systematic time delay in order to account for the misalignment of what is happening in the brain and what is happening in consciousness shown by the beta phenomenon. For us to experience events as happening in a specific order, it is not necessary that information about these enters the brain in the same order.

The rejection of the self as the substantial centre of our mental world is no recent philosophical phenomenon. It goes back two and a half millennia when the historical Buddha in ancient India described the theory of non-self.



According to this theory, we consist of a body and four psychological components, corresponding to different cognitive functions. The self cannot be identified with any one of them (since all of them change frequently, while the self is supposed to be continuous), nor can it just be the collection of all of them (since the self is a unified, single thing, not a coalition of shifting elements). Nor is the self a separately existent thing, distinct from the four components. This does not imply that talk of selves and persons should be eliminated; these form an important part of how we conceptualize the world. But the self has nothing more than a strictly nominal existence. It is superimposed on our physical and mental constituents for purely practical purposes. It allows us to locate ourselves in the world, rather like the pointer of our mouse allows us to locate ourselves within the interface of our computer. But like the pointer that is neither 'in' the computer, nor a continuous object (when we switch off the computer, there is no pointer), nor constituting the substantial

### Excerpt from the *Mahāpuṇṇama Sutta*

'Monks, what do you think? Is matter permanent or impermanent?' – 'Impermanent, venerable sir.' – 'Is what is impermanent suffering or happiness?' – 'Suffering, venerable sir.' – 'Is what is impermanent, suffering, and subject to change fit to be regarded thus? *This is mine, this I am, this is my self?*' – 'No, venerable sir.'

'Monks, what do you think: Are feeling, perception, reaction and consciousness permanent or impermanent?' – 'Impermanent, venerable sir.' – 'Is what is impermanent suffering or happiness?' – 'Suffering, venerable sir.' – 'Is what is impermanent, suffering, and subject to change fit to be regarded thus? *This is mine, this I am, this is my self?*' – 'No, venerable sir.'

'Therefore, Monks, any kind of matter whatsoever, whether past, future, or present, should be seen as it actually is with proper wisdom thus: *This is not mine, I am not this, this is not my self*. Any kind of feeling, perception, reaction, and consciousness whatever should be seen as it actually is, by proper wisdom thus: *This is not mine, this I am not, this is not my self.*'



centre of the computer's workings, the self is not what it appears to be.

When we say that the self is superimposed on the constituents, the question arises: 'Who does the superimposing?' When considering the self as the unifier of our experiential world, it makes sense to understand it along the lines of a pilot in a flight simulator. From a range of perceptual input, our brain creates the image of the world in which the self operates. We cannot step outside of our brain, so we have no way of finding out what the world beyond the intracranial simulation is like. To us, it does not even feel like a simulation. But the problems with the Cartesian theatre suggest that there is no pilot, no self, for whose benefit the simulation is put on. Rather, the collection of our physical and mental constituents acts like a *total* flight simulator that not only simulates the information received in the cockpit, but simulates the pilot as well. The self as the unifier of our perceptual input is a simulation or illusion, yet there is no non-simulated or non-illusory someone experiencing the simulation or having the illusion.

It is interesting to note that the unified self also comes under attack from a somewhat unexpected direction, namely a particular interpretation of quantum physics.



We recall that according to some interpretations the collapse of the wave function happens when consciousness interacts with the quantum object to be measured. This interaction, the measurement, then determines which of the several possible properties the quantum object *could* have is the actual one. After the measurement, the object will have only this property and none of the others. Yet the interpretation that concerns us here claims that after the measurement, *all* the different possible properties are properties the quantum object actually has. Because nothing can have different incompatible properties at the same time, this implies that when the object is observed, the universe splits into a set of near-duplicates, the first continuing on its course with the quantum object having one property, the second with its having another property, and so forth. This is the cosmic equivalent of the labyrinthine novel of Tsu'i Pen described by Borges, where every choice of the protagonist spawns several further narratives, one for each possible outcome. In this continuously branching tree of possibilities, everything that could happen is indeed described in some narrative.

This so-called 'many worlds interpretation' allows us to interpret crucial physical experiments without having to assume a fundamental difference between mind and matter. On the other hand, since we, as observers, are material objects as well, processes of measurement also split *us*, so that there will be separate *mes* continuing their existence in separate universes, never again to be united. It is as if on rolling a die, not only will you get a particular number, but five complete universes come into existence at the same time, each containing a you having just thrown a die with one of the five remaining numbers.

But which of these six selves is you? If each of them is a continuation of you, you cannot have a unified self, since the six selves will develop in very different directions, have different experiences, and make different choices, while a single self is supposed to develop only in one direction, have one set of experiences, and make one kind of choices. If one of them is you, on the other hand, it seems as if you are immortal.

Consider the following experiment. Take a device which measures some property of a quantum object. The property can either be present or absent, and the probability of each is the same. Now hook up this measuring device with a gun. Every minute the device measures a different quantum object and does nothing if the property to be measured is absent. If it is present, on the other hand, the measuring device triggers the gun and shoots you in the head. If you run this experiment, it should appear to you as if the gun never fires, for every time it does the universe splits into two, and in one of these the measured property is absent, and the gun does not fire. The continuation of you is the self in the world in which the gun does not fire, rather than the dead self in the world where the gun does fire. (If you observe *someone else* running the experiment, on the other hand, there is a 50% chance that you will see them dead after the first minute.) As long as the probability of the measured property being absent is not zero, you could survive a scenario like this indefinitely. The same point obviously applies outside the experiment as well. As the splitting of worlds takes place all the time, as long as there is a world in which you are alive that is the result of some such split just before your death, you will continue to be alive in this world, and since the 'you' in this world is the real you, you will never experience your own death.

Despite the fact that this kind of immortality might appear attractive to some, the idea that exactly one of the countless universes branching at every moment contains you is somewhat problematic. A key difficulty is to answer *why* our self is to be found in the world in which the die comes up six, rather than in the one where it comes up five. What determines which self is going to be our continuation? In all six versions, we have near-identical bodies, so it cannot be any physical difference that determines which world our self is in. The only way to solve this difficulty seems to consist in postulating an imperceptible, non-physical self. But if there is such a self, we immediately ask ourselves whether it could have been the case that something went wrong somewhere and that even though we *think* our self is now in the present world, it is really in some other world that split off this one a long time ago.



Somehow this does not appear to be a situation we should worry about. We seem to be getting back to the situation of the self-destroying drug discussed earlier. If the imperceptible self is only postulated in order to ensure the existence of a continuant through the splitting universes of the many worlds interpretation, we might save ourselves groundless worries about our self being really where we think it is by giving up the underlying assumption that there is such a unified self in the first place.

Our final intuitive view of our self is that it is the locus of control. The self is the agent that transforms information received from the world into actions on the world. The core of our conception of agenthood is the ability to carry out actions that are no direct consequences of perceptual input. Passing the salt when requested to do so is an action very different in kind from reaching for the

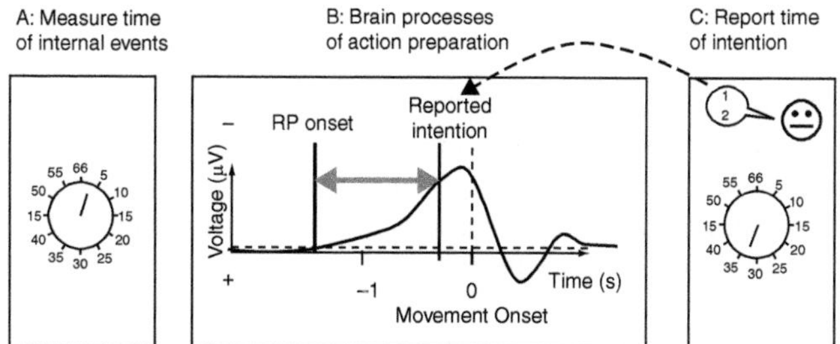


**13. Exploring the readiness potential (RP)**

salt yourself, prompted only by your own desire for salt on your food. It is intriguing that this central portion of agenthood looks very different when we pay close attention to the mechanics of the human brain.

When studying the activity of the brain's motor cortex that leads to voluntary muscle movements, scientists discovered a particular pattern of neuronal activity that precedes these movements, the so-called 'readiness potential'. In the 1980s, the neuroscientist Benjamin Libet conducted a widely discussed experiment investigating the temporal relation between this readiness potential and the conscious decision to act. Subjects were asked to perform a hand movement at a time of their own choosing while watching a moving dial. The electrical activity of their brain was measured with an electro-encephalogram (EEG), and the subjects were asked to report where the pointer of the dial was when they first felt the *intention* to move their hand. Interestingly enough, the time reported was consistently later than the beginning of the readiness potential in the brain. It is therefore hard to see how the intention could have caused the readiness potential, as the experience of willing a certain action only begins after the brain events that bring the action into being. The intention to act appears to manifest spontaneously in our mind, yet it does have a causal precursor which we are not aware of. This precursor, the readiness potential, is introspectively invisible to us, but exists nevertheless. The intention to move our hand merely appears spontaneous and uncaused because it is the first link in a chain of brain processes that crosses the border from the unconscious to the conscious. In this particular experimental set-up, both the appearance of willing the action and the action itself arise from the brain, yet we infer that it is the willing that is causally responsible for the action.

Our mind's tendency to manufacture the appearance of intentional action even if there is none can also be observed in other contexts. The mere fact that an action appears to us as being the exclusive result of our intention to act does not guarantee that this is in fact so. Brain activity can be triggered or suppressed by letting magnetic fields act on the brain through the skull through a technique called transcranial magnetic stimulation. It is then possible to devise an experiment in which subjects are asked to choose to lift their right or left index finger after a certain signal. At the same time, magnetic stimulation is applied to the motor area of the brain. Subjects are more likely to lift the finger of the hand opposite to the area of the brain stimulated but were not aware that their choice was influenced by a force outside of their heads.



In even more extreme cases, our mind can confabulate an intention for an action that has not been brought about by us at all. In an interesting experiment the subject was asked to pick out pictures on a computer screen using a computer mouse they shared, ouija-board style, with a confederate. Via headphones, they would hear words, some of which related to objects on the screen. In fact, the 'confederate' was one of the experimenters and would force the mouse gently towards a picture without the subject noticing. If the subject's mouse was directed to the picture of a rose, and they heard the word 'rose' some seconds before this on their headphones, the subjects reported feeling that they acted intentionally in moving the mouse there. The thought of a rose is triggered by purely external causes (the headphones), yet its occurrence enhances the appearance of intentional mental causation. The mind produces an 'I did this' narrative which we then regard as an indubitable first-person report, despite its lacking any factual basis.

Doubt about the self as the locus of control not only arises from the detailed study of how the hardware underlying our minds works, but from a somewhat unexpected direction: memetics. Memetics, the study of memes, is an extrapolation from genetics, the study of genes. Genetics studies how biological life develops by the replication of genes, memetics how the development of the life of the mind can be understood by the replication of non-material idea-like replicators, the memes. A meme can be as basic as the idea of boiling food before eating it, or of transporting loads by means of wheels, or it can constitute a highly complex structure of ideas like the game of Go, Euclidean geometry, Pāṇini's Sanskrit grammar, perspectival drawing, and, of course, memetics itself. Genes are invisible objects that are carried by a host (the organism that has the gene) and provide specific effects (the organism's phenotype). Memes are similarly invisible, carried by individual minds, and have specific effects determining what happens to that mind in the long run.

An influential idea in contemporary evolutionary theory is that it is not organisms, but genes that are in the driving seat. Rather than viewing genes as the organism's tool for reproducing, thereby enhancing its fitness, genes are regarded as selfish replicators that bring about an organism to raise their chances of getting themselves copied. While it is often the case that what is good for the gene is also good for the host (a gene conferring immunity against a common disease, for example, will have greater chances of replicating, since its host is likely to live longer), quite dramatic conflicts can occur.

These are particularly evident in the case of so-called segregation distorter genes, which do not influence such features as hair or skin colour, but the very process of cell division that halves the chromosomes and produces sperm and egg cells. The segregation distorters make sure that they are over-represented in the sperm and egg cells, and thereby tremendously increase their chances of replicating. They even do this when the consequences for the individual organism or the population of organisms carrying the gene are disastrous. A well-known example, the t-gene in mice, that cheats on other genes in this way, has no major effects on the organism if it is only inherited from one parent. If it is inherited from *both* parents, however, the resulting mouse either dies young or is sterile. As the t-gene spreads through a population aided by its ability to have itself over-represented in sperm and egg cells, the likelihood of any baby mouse inheriting the t-gene from both father and mother increases. Eventually, an entire population of mice carrying the t-gene can become extinct in this way. Not only does this gene work against the interests of the organisms carrying it, it also demonstrates a remarkable lack of foresight by working against its own interests.



In the same way as the genes congregated in an organism to replicate better, memes, we might think, got together to form a self. We see a similar inversion of the familiar order of priority here – it's not us having the ideas, it's the ideas having us. According to this view, the self is an artefact made by memes that colonize a human brain so as to make the reproduction of memes easier. In the same way as genes come together in an organism to make their reproduction easier (because some genes can control the production of biological components required by other genes), memes congregating in a self have an easier time getting themselves copied. In such a self, memes that can help each other to be reproduced can congregate. The meme for making gunpowder spreads better when it forms part of a self that also contains the memes for bombs, incendiaries, rockets, mines, guns, and cannons. It would therefore be mistaken to assume that the memes had by us are there because they correspond to the way the world is, or because they make us smarter, or more compassionate, or more successful; it is simply because they are advantageous to themselves, that is, because they are good at replicating. As in the case of genes, the question whether a replicator is good for the host is not a very useful criterion for assessing its success.

Yet it would be wrong to think of our self as being taken over by parasitic memes. It is because memes play an essential role in bringing our selves into being that any opposition of memes versus 'us' is misplaced. There is no independent mind struggling to fight off an invasion of alien memes, but only one complex of memes that regards itself as a self, and regards other memes either as allies to take on board or as intruders to repel. Of course, things do not appear to us in this way, we believe that we are in control, that it is us having the ideas, rather than the other way round. Cognitive science sometimes describes such cognitive artefacts as the self as 'transparent' – we see right through them without noticing their constructed nature. Something similar holds for our visual field, which appears continuous and uniform, even though it is anything but, since different parts of our retina have vastly different powers of resolution, since each eye contains a blindspot, and since our eyes continuously jump around in a succession of movements known as saccades. The construction of a continuous field from these jumpy and partial data is not cognitively available to us, in the same way as the production of our self by a congregation of memes is not anything we could perceive. The self is an illusion without being anybody who has the illusion.

If, as the preceding considerations show, our intuitive conception of our self as an unchanging agent and unifier inside of our bodies is less plausible than it appears, where does this leave us regarding the reality of the self? Clearly, its reality according to the Matrix and 1984 definition cannot be challenged. Our self appears to us – due to its very transparency – and most people also perceive that most other people have selves. But its reality according to Johnson's definition is not apparent. The self is not something that is not made up. It is a cognitive model and, if certain memeticists are right, it is a complex made up from congregating memes. The apocalyptic definition is obviously not applicable; there would be no selves if we were not around. We have also seen that the reality of the self is not evident in terms of one of the most substantial definitions of reality, the turtle definition. The various primitives assumed by theories that attempt to provide a comprehensive account of key portions of the world – elementary particles, genes, memes – do not include selves among them. The self, it appears, is nothing that appears at a fundamental level of description, but an artefact that arises when various simple factors come together in a complex whole.

# Chapter 4
# Is time real?

In a range of hills to the east of the River Rhine lie the ruins of a Cistercian monastery, Heisterbach Abbey. Local legends relate the story of a monk from the 15th century who wandered from the monastery into the surrounding woods, contemplating Psalm 90:4 ('For a thousand years in thy sight are but as yesterday when it is past, and as a watch in the night'). Sitting down in the forest, the monk fell asleep and awoke only when the monastery's bell called for the evening prayer. As he returned, the monastery appeared strangely changed to him, and when he entered the chapel, none of the monks recognized him. They asked him who he was, and he replied that his name was Ivo, and that he entered the monastery in the same year that Engelbert von Berg became Archbishop of Cologne. 'But this is more than three hundred years ago!', the brothers said. The monk suddenly felt the weight of three centuries weigh down his shoulders, and just before he died, he understood that God had shown him His existence outside of time, and had now brought him back into it.

Expressed in this legend, we find the doubt that time as we experience it may not be real according to the apocalyptic definition. Our time, human time, it seems to claim, is a distinctly human thing, something that would not be there if humans were not. Beyond it is another kind of time, an objectively real but

**14. Ruins of Heisterbach Abbey**



fundamentally different kind of time, the eternal presence of the unchanging existence of God.

A more severe doubt, the doubt that time is not even a fundamental, irreducible feature of the world (that is, that it is also not real according to the turtle definition), is surprisingly common amongst both philosophers and scientists. The Cambridge philosopher John McTaggart Ellis, one of the best-known proponents of the unreality of time, pointed out that we tend to think of time in two radically different ways. On the one hand, time is *dynamic*, and every moment changes from first being future, then becoming present, and finally, once it is over, moving into the past. On the other hand, temporal properties can also be regarded as *unmoving*, when we think of one moment being before or after another, or of two moments being simultaneous. Such relations do not change as moments move from future, through the present, into the past. The 5th of January is always before the 6th of January of any given year, whether this year is past, present, or future. McTaggart referred to the first way of thinking about time as the A-series, and to the second as the B-series (if you have trouble remembering which is which, think of the 'a' in 'dynamic'). The B-series, McTaggart argues, is not sufficient for an understanding of what time is. Time involves change, and in the B-series nothing changes. The 'before', 'after', and 'at the same time' relations between moments are eternally fixed, like a sequence of rooms, one after the other, and will never change. In addition, we definitely know more about time than just information about the B-series. Some being that knew all B-theoretic facts would know the temporal relations between all moments, but would not be able to tell you today's date, as he would not be able to say when the present moment is. The concept of the present does not form part of the B-theoretic vocabulary, it only occurs in the A-series. But the A-series, McTaggart points out, has problems of its own.

No event can be both past and present, or present and future, or past and future. Yet time understood according to the A-series implies that as time elapses every event will have all three incompatible properties of past, present, and future. So the A-series is contradictory.



The solution to this difficulty seems simple: point out that no event has the properties of being past, present, or future *at the same time* but only in succession. *First* it is future, *then* present, and *after that*, past. But it is not entirely clear how to spell out this intuitively convincing response in detail. Take a specific event, such as McTaggart's birthday (let us call this M). It looks as if we could defuse the contradiction by saying that M is future in 1850 and past in 1900. But the pieces of time-talk used here ('future in 1850', 'past in 1900') are no longer A-theoretic expressions, since they do not change as time progresses. What was future in 1850 will remain future, no matter how time develops. Avoiding the contradiction by rephrasing dynamic A-theoretic descriptions as B-theoretic ones does not really help, since we already saw above that the B-theoretic account of time was not satisfactory.

Another idea would be to get rid of the contradiction by specifying A-series descriptions using more A-series descriptions. M, we could argue, does not have inconsistent temporal properties because

> M is past *in the present,*
> M is present *in the past,*
> M is future *in the distant past.*

Not only are these descriptions compatible with each other, unlike descriptions such as 'future in 1850', they also change with the passage of time. As time progresses, M will change from being present *in the past* to being present *in the distant past.* The problem is that when we are talking about time, we don't just talk about the present, we also talk about the past. For example, it is a past fact *now* that the Battle of Hastings is presently taking place. Some examples of what are past facts now about McTaggart's birthday in 1866 include



> M is past *in the recent past,*
> M is present *in the near future,*
> M is future *in the present.*

Unfortunately, these facts are not compatible with the A-series descriptions we have just given (for example, M cannot be past in the present *and* future in the present). We are once again faced with a contradiction. As the B-series does not really capture the essence of time, and as the A-series gives rise to inconsistencies, McTaggart concludes that time is not real. When we perceive time, we perceive an illusion.

A similar view was held by Kurt Gödel, one of the greatest mathematicians of the 20th century, and perhaps of all time. Gödel pointed out that an objective flow of time, time understood according to the A-series, has to imply that reality, understood as everything there is, grows in time. As time passes, merely future things come into existence and enlarge the set of everything there is, adding layer by layer of sediments of present moments that then quickly become past. The birthday cake I want to bake tomorrow does not exist yet, but as the birthday moves from future to present, the cake turns from a mere potential, future object into an actual, present object. Reality now contains one more thing it did not contain before, namely the birthday cake.

One difficulty with this is that our best present physical theories, in particular the special theory of relativity, do not allow us to speak of a 'now' in any absolute sense any more. Consider a simple example. Assume a flash of light illuminates a moving railway carriage through a window at the middle of the carriage. At each end of the carriage is a mirror, and since each is exactly the same distance from the window, an observer in the carriage will see the light being reflected from both the mirrors at the same time. Yet to an observer *outside* of the carriage, the light appears to reach one of the mirrors before the other, since one of the mirrors is moving towards the approaching light as the carriage is moving, while the other is moving away from it. We therefore have to say that the very same two events (light hitting each of the two mirrors) are simultaneous for one observer, but not simultaneous for another. It is thus impossible to snap our fingers now and claim that there is any objective way in which we can refer to the set of all events happening at the same time as the snap, that is, all the events that happen in the absolute now. From our perspective, the snap and some other events (the chiming of the clock, the vibrating of the bell) all occur at the same time, but for a different observer they might form a sequence.



But this means that there is no objective fact about which objects are part of the growing reality, and which are not. Everything that exists now is such a part, but whose 'now' are we talking about? We seem to be pushed towards saying that not only simultaneity is relative to an observer within an inertial frame, but reality is as well, since my now may contain different things than your now.

Yet such a view of reality is difficult to reconcile with its most fundamental understandings in terms of the apocalyptic or turtle definition. If what is real is what is there no matter what, or what remains if we follow down the chain of dependence from molecules to atoms, subatomic particles, and beyond, that this something is relative to an observer does not seem to be an option. Many thinkers, Gödel amongst them, have therefore preferred to save the notion of absolute reality by rejecting the idea of an objective flow of time, of a reality that grows as a merely potential future moves into an actual present.

Gödel also defended this conclusion by a particularly interesting argument attempting to show that in a specific class of universes with special physical conditions, it is possible to make a round trip on a rocket that takes us into any direction of time, past or future, and back again, in the same way as our universe allows us to travel into any direction of space. It is clear that in such a 'Gödel universe' allowing time travel, there could not be an objective flow of time, an expanding and growing reality, since we cannot travel somewhere that does not exist. The imaginary island of Laputa is not a potential travel destination in our world, since it does not exist. For the same reason, future (and, some might argue, past) times are no such destinations, since these do not exist either. But in the Gödel universe, travel to the future is possible, so the future must exist. But this means that reality cannot grow as future becomes present, since everything that exists is already part of reality.

Whether our world is in fact such a 'Gödel universe' is not essential for Gödel's view of time. What is essential, however, is that a Gödel universe differs from ours at most in the way matter and motion are distributed on a cosmic scale; it is not governed by different laws of nature. Whether there is an objective flow of time or not, on the other hand, is a question of what kind of laws hold in a world, and not a question of where different particles of matter are located. Not only do facts about the distribution of matter and motion appear to be too weak to bring about the flow of time, establishing whether these facts hold, and thereby establishing whether or not we live in a Gödel universe, is a very intricate undertaking. It requires sophisticated measurements by powerful telescopes, together with very complex chains of theoretical derivations. Thus my belief that time flows, and that tomorrow's birthday cake really comes into existence only tomorrow, would depend on the outcome of these very complex observations. But something seems to have gone wrong here, as it appears to imply that the flow of time is a kind of thing such that direct experience would not be conclusive evidence for its presence. The kind of time the existence of which could be guaranteed by these observations would have nothing to do with the time as it appears to us: whether or not it exists, the world would look just the same. It would not even be clear why we would want to call it time at all, rather than, say, 'the way matter and motion are distributed on a cosmic scale'.



The laws of nature cannot establish the flow of time (since they are the same in the Gödel universe and in our world, and time only flows in the former), nor can the mere appearance of time (since this does not differ in the two worlds), nor can the distribution of motion and matter (since these are wholly removed from our direct experience of time). We therefore have to conclude, Gödel argues, that there is no such thing. The existence of a flowing time and of a gradually increasing reality is an illusion.

Besides the flow of time, there are other temporal features that initially appear extremely obvious but on closer consideration turn out to be considerably less so. Times come in three flavours, past, present, and future. If we ask ourselves whether time is real, we have to specify which (if any) of these three parts of time is real.

Three possibilities are discussed most often. All agree that the present is real. The Growing Universe theory, which we have just discussed, claims that the future is not real, and postulates a

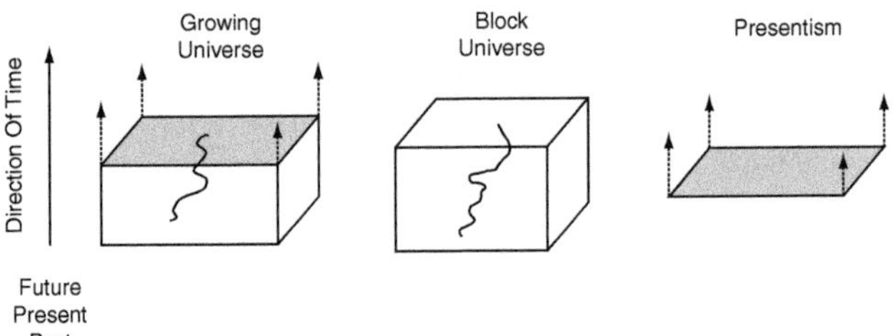


**15. Three views of time. The present is marked in light grey**

genuine flow of time into an open future. The Block Universe theory, on the other hand, supported by the Gödelian arguments just presented, claims that all three divisions of time are equally real, and that the idea of a flowing time and growing reality is an illusion. A musical analogy might make things clearer here: the flowing now that is part of the Growing Universe theory corresponds to the flow of a piece of music as it is played. The fixing of the piece into a musical score, where all its parts are present at once corresponds to the geometricizing of time into the space-time of the Block Universe theory. (The final alternative, presentism, which holds that only the present is real, will be discussed below.)



The Growing Universe theory seems to mirror the view of time most people have. They regard the past as real (at least to some extent), take the present to be real, and the future to be undecided and hence unreal. The notions of reality in play here are Johnson's definition and the apocalyptic definition. Neither the past nor the present are something we can make up; the past is gone, complete and unalterable, and the present is something we have to deal with in the way it is, not in the way we would like it to be. Solely the future is open and indeterminate, it alone can be formed by us more or less according to our will. The past is also real according to the apocalyptic definition. Even if all conscious minds now vanished from the world, the past would still be the past.

The reality of the past appears to be a direct consequence of our inability to change any aspect of it. What has happened has happened in a certain way, and it will eternally remain the case that it has

**Felix Eberty, *The Stars and the Earth, or Thoughts upon Space, Time, and Eternity* (1854)**

An observer in Centaur can, of course, never see the northern hemisphere of the earth, because this constellation never rises above our horizon. But supposing it possible, and that an observer were standing in this star with such powerful vision as to be able to distinguish all particulars upon our little earth, shining feebly luminous in its borrowed light, he would see, in the year 1843, the public illumination which in the year 1840, made the cities of our native country shine with the brightness of day during the darkness of night. An observer in Vega would see what happened with us twelve years ago; and so on, until an inhabitant of a star of the twelfth magnitude, if we imagine him with unlimited power of vision contemplating the earth, sees it as it was four thousand years ago, when Memphis was founded, and the patriarch Abraham wandered upon its surface.

In the immeasurably great number of fixed stars which are scattered about in the universe, floating in ether at a distance between fifteen and twenty billion miles from us, reckoning backwards any given number of years, doubtless a star could be found which sees the past epochs of our earth as if existing now, or so nearly corresponding to the time, that the observer need wait no long time to see its condition at the required moment. [...]

The pictures of all secret deeds, which have ever been transacted, remain indissolubly and indelibly for ever, reaching from one sun beyond another. Not only upon the floor of the chamber is the blood-spot of murder indelibly fixed, but the deed glances further and further into spacious heaven.

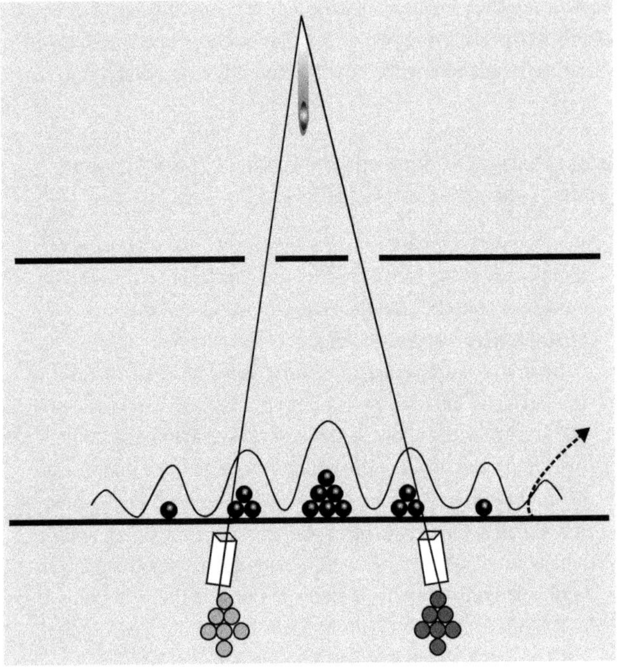

**16. Delayed-choice experiment**

happened in this way. Something that puts up so much resistance to our intentions and desires must exist independent of us. Yet it is interesting to note that (as Bertrand Russell pointed out), for all we can tell, the world might have been created five minutes ago, together with all its fossils, archaeological remains, archives, libraries, buildings, and memories. We would tell exactly the same stories about the past as we do now, but they would indeed be just stories, since none of the past times they seem to refer to actually exist. When we talk about the past, we are really speaking in a convoluted sense about the present, about the fossils and remains we find now, the documents we read now, the memories that arise in our mind now.

Less radical proposals that deny the reality of only part of the past have been put forward by historians, most notably the Phantom Time Hypothesis, claiming that the years between 614 and 911 were an invention by later medieval historians. According to this view, all buildings or artefacts from this period have to be dated to different times, Charlemagne (742–814) was a fictional character, and the year 2000 was really the year 1703. Fantastic as these ideas may sound, they are still relatively tame when compared to the consequences of a well-known thought experiment in quantum physics.

In this so-called 'delayed-choice experiment', we shoot a quantum object at a barrier with two slits in it. If the object behaves like a particle, it will go through one of the two slits; if it behaves like a wave, it will show the familiar interference pattern on the other side of the barrier. Beyond the barrier is a detection mechanism like a phosphor screen, and behind this screen are two telescopes, each aimed at one slit. If the screen is in place, the quantum objects will accumulate in accordance with the interference pattern; if the screen is removed, they will be observed by the telescopes as coming either through the left or the right slit. So far, so familiar.



Things become peculiar when we decide whether to leave the screen in place, or whether to lift it in favour of the telescopes only *after* the quantum object has passed through the barrier. By this time, it will already have been decided whether the quantum object went through one slit (like a particle) or through both at once (like a wave). It should therefore be possible that the quantum object goes through both slits at once, and we select the telescope detection mechanism, thereby observing the object through both telescopes. Yet such a situation never happens.

This result can be made more dramatic by substituting a distant galaxy for the barrier with the two slits. Being very massive objects, galaxies have the ability to bend space-time, so that a beam of light will be deflected by them. We can now imagine such a galaxy being located between us and a light source. The photons originating from this source will be deflected and will either go round the galaxy on the left, on the right, or they will go round both sides simultaneously. Again, which path they take seems to be determined by the measuring device we choose. Yet the light we look at is billions of years old, and would have decided which path to take long before human beings existed anywhere on this earth. This experiment seems to imply that our decision in the present (to raise or not to raise the screen) determines the events that happened in the past (which way round the photon went). It certainly is not the case that we could just change *any* fact about the past in this way (for example, we cannot now make it true that the photon took the left-hand path). But even if there are just some aspects of the past we can change in the present, arguments for the reality of the past on the grounds of its unalterable nature and the resistance it puts up to our desires look remarkably shaky.



While theories denying the reality of the past are certainly very much at odds with our usual view of the world, the irreality of the future is regarded as intuitively uncontroversial by most people. If the future already *was* real (it is argued), and was not *made* real by what we do in the present, our actions would have little purpose. The defender of the Block Universe theory, it seems, has a tough time defending free will. According to this view, moving into the future would be rather like walking through a series of dark rooms, carrying a candle: as the light of the present shines on them, previously hidden objects come into view. Yet there is no doubt that these objects had been there all along.

Given the intuitive plausibility of the irreality of the future, it is somewhat surprising that an argument for its reality can be made on the basis of another widely held theory, namely the theory of relativity.

The above example of the mirrors in the moving railway carriage has shown that two events that are simultaneous for one observer are not so for another observer moving relative to the first one. If the distances involved are large, even a small difference in relative speed between the observers can result in a considerable lack of synchronicity. This fact is exploited in the so-called Andromeda paradox.

The Andromeda galaxy is about 2.5 million light years away from the earth. If we want to find out which event on Andromeda is simultaneous with which event on earth (for example, with a digital clock jumping from 11:59:59 to 12:00:00), we have to be very careful about how fast the clock is moving. Events on Andromeda simultaneous with my stationary wristwatch switching from one second before noon to noon, and events simultaneous with my friend's watch doing so, will be about an earth day apart, if my friend is just walking at the leisurely pace of one foot per second.

Now here is where things start to get strange. Assume evil aliens somewhere in the Andromeda galaxy decide to attack earth. They reach their decision at the same time as my watch switches to noon. I can see my friend strolling along the lawn, and as his watch switches to noon, events on Andromeda have already advanced by one earth day: the intergalactic fleet is already on its way to destroy earth. My friend and I are both real, and it seems uncontroversial that what is simultaneous with something real is also real. Thus both events on Andromeda must be real, but one event happens an earth day later than the other. Events in the future, it appears, can be as real as the present.

We can generalize this point by showing that for any event, past, present, or future, we can define a location such that if a person was moving with a certain speed at that location, this event would be simultaneous with him. There might not actually be such a person, but it still remains peculiar that whether or not some future event was real depends on who moves where in the universe with what speed!

It seems that we are left with two equally strange alternatives. The first is to believe that parts of the future are already laid out in a fixed way, and not some fluid collections of mere possibilities that can be shaped by our actions. These are the parts where there exists an observer's frame of reference somewhere in the universe such that that particular part of the future is simultaneous with him. The second alternative is to hold that not just simultaneity is observer-relative, but that reality is as well. The approaching fleet from Andromeda is real for my friend (since it is simultaneous with him), and my friend is real for me, but the approaching fleet is not real for me, since it is located in my future. There is no shared, objective, observer-independent present reality, but only a real-for-me, real-for-you, and so on. These subjective realities can overlap. (The approaching fleet from Andromeda is real for my friend, and he is also real for himself. Only the friend, but not the approaching fleet, is also real for me.) The reality we all live in would therefore not be all there is, but just that small part of reality in which we can all interact with each other, since all objects and events in this part are real for each and every one of us.



Finally, what about the present? Of the three divisions of time, this seems to have the greatest claim to being real. As opposed to

**St Augustine, *Confessions*, Book 11**

> But what now is manifest and clear is, that neither are there future nor past things. Nor is it fitly said, There are three times, past, present and future; but perchance it might be fitly said, There are three times; a present of things past, a present of things present, and a present of things future. For these three do somehow exist in the soul, and otherwise I see them not: present of things past, memory; present of things present, sight; present of things future, expectation. If of these things we are permitted to speak, I see three times, and I grant there are three.

the past and the future, this is where we lead our lives. It is also what we share with all other beings: we are all in different places, but we are all at the same time. As St Augustine points out, the only reality we can give to the past is the traces it left in the present, and the only reality we can give to the future are our present expectations.

Yet for all its apparent solidity, the present seems to be considerably more difficult to grasp than the past or future. With either of these, it is evident that they lasted (or will last) for a long time. But how long does the present last? No matter how short a duration we pick, we always seem to be able to distinguish further temporal parts in this, and of these only the middle parts properly deserve to be called 'the present'. But if we keep dividing time in this way, the present shrinks to a mere razor's edge, bounded by the past on one side and by the future on the other. This new 'present' is so short that we wonder how anything could happen in it at all!



At this point, it is useful to distinguish the subjective or psychological present moment from the true present. We can easily determine the duration of the subjective present moment by experimenting with a metronome. If we set this at 120 beats per minute (so that we hear two beats every second), we can form groups of these beats by giving an additional subjective weight to every second beat we hear. Larger groups can be formed by giving such weight to every third beat, every fourth beat, and so on. Yet this ability to form groups breaks down somewhere. This is easy to see when we reduce the speed to 40 beats per minute. Now the beats are 1.5 seconds apart, and it is already difficult to form groups of two. In general, human beings are unable to form subjectively experienced groups of beats that last longer than three seconds. (If you try reciting poetry with a stopwatch, you will also realize that the spoken duration of most verses is less than three seconds.) It is therefore sensible to estimate the duration of the subjective present as lasting for about three seconds.

The subjective or psychological present is thus no razor's edge, but a saddleback with a width of its own. But the psychological present is, of course, not the same as the true present. Even though the psychological present constitutes our temporal horizon, including all the events we consider to be happening simultaneously and to be happening *now*, it can still be subdivided further. A man walking at normal speed traverses a distance of about four metres during the subjective present. When he reaches the midway point, the last two metres he walked will be located in the part of the psychological present that is really past, while the next two metres are in the part that is really future. The subjective or appearing present is temporally extended, and divisible into earlier and later parts. The true present, on the other hand, contains no parts and has no duration.

When we ask whether the present is real, we do not just want to know whether it is real according to the relatively 'soft' first three definitions of 'real'. We all know that the present appears to us, and also appears to most people, so its reality according to the Matrix definition and the 1984 definition is beyond dispute. But what about the 'hard' apocalyptic and turtle definitions?



A difficulty we face when arguing for the reality of the present moment in these senses is that it does not feature in scientific theories at all. While the present is tremendously important for the way the world appears to us (because it is *when* the world appears to us), it does not have any claim to reality according to the apocalyptic understanding of the term. If there were no conscious beings, there would be no 'now'. A complete scientific description of the universe would not tell us when now is. It does not endow the present moment with any special quality not shared by any of the other temporal moments.

Another difficulty is that despite all its subjective importance, we do not ever seem to experience the present moment. The processing of neural information takes time. If you feel the warmth of the fire with your hand, this perception has to travel from a particular part of your skin along various neural pathways up your arm, through your body, until it finally reaches the brain. Once the information about the temperature has arrived there, it is integrated with various other pieces of information (that may have entered via your sense organs at different times), such as the sight of the flame, or the smell of burning wood. This complex coherent representation involving objects or events and their properties will be the representation of a burning fire. Yet once this information is cognitively available to us, the moment that gave rise to it, and everything that happened during that moment, is already a thing of the past. When trying to connect with the present moment, we face the same situation as someone looking at a distant star, the light of which still reaches his eyes, while the star itself has long ceased to be. The timescale involved here is obviously much shorter, but the fundamental point remains the same.

The time delay involved when our brain builds a conscious representation of the present was investigated by the American physiologist Benjamin Libet in a set of experiments beginning in the 1950s. Libet's experiments are particularly interesting because they involved direct interaction with a subject's brain. Certain kinds of surgery have to be carried out while the patient is conscious and only locally anaesthetized. In this way, the surgeon can stimulate specific areas on the surface of the brain using a weak electric current. Observing the patient's bodily reactions and responses, the surgeon can then produce a map of the brain's surface, making sure that all vital areas are avoided during the subsequent surgery. While the mapping is carried out, it is sometimes possible to perform additional experiments that do not introduce any new risks (assuming the patient agrees to this).

Libet experimented with stimulating parts of the brain that process tactile information coming from the skin. By applying an electric current to these areas, the patient feels a sensation, which is then 'projected outwards' to that part of the body where the sensory information processed by that part of the brain normally comes from. Even though he has his brain stimulated, the patient feels a tingling on the skin of his hand, not on the surface of his brain.

One interesting result Libet discovered is that the electric impulse has to be applied for a relatively long time (about half a second) before the patient perceives it. When looking at perceptual processes, 500 milliseconds is surprisingly long. (For comparison, the 'transmission time' necessary for an impulse travelling from the hand to the brain is only about 20 milliseconds.) Shorter electric stimulations had no effect, nor would it help to simply make the impulses more intense. It is important to note that this half-second perceptual delay does not imply that all our interaction with the world lags half a second behind. We are able to react much faster than that. (For example, we can distinguish sounds as little as three milliseconds apart.) Yet most of our very fast reactions do not involve any awareness of what we are reacting to. As far as our conscious perception of the world is concerned, a 500-millisecond delay appears to be necessary before a sensation becomes conscious. Unconscious detection of content by the brain is possibly faster, but awareness takes time.



This half-second delay may be compared to the delay customary when broadcasting 'live' television (which can range from several seconds to several minutes). This allows for last-minute editing or censorship after some event is filmed, but before it is broadcast. (Such a delay was famously absent during the 'wardrobe malfunction' at the 2004 Super Bowl halftime show.) Something similar can happen in the brain: in the 500 milliseconds it takes for a skin sensation to become conscious, it is possible to 'edit it out', so that it never enters experience at all. Libet introduced his patients to two sensations, one caused by stimulation of the skin, and one caused by stimulation of the brain. Both could be easily distinguished when experienced separately. But curiously enough, if the brain stimulation took place about 200 milliseconds after the skin stimulation, the skin stimulation would not be felt at all.

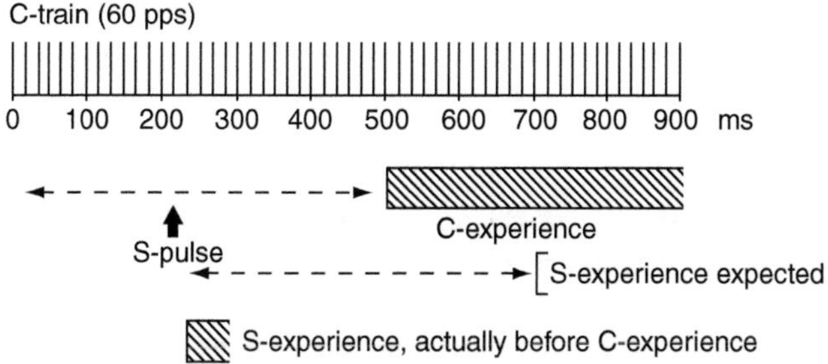


**17. Set-up of Libet's experiment**

The brain stimulation managed to mask the skin sensation, thereby preventing it from entering consciousness. This is only possible because our perception does not put us in direct contact with the present. By the time we become conscious of some sensation, it is already half a second old, and because of the temporal thickness of the process of perception, it is possible to interfere with a signal that has already reached our brain, making it disappear just before it enters consciousness. In the case of supposedly live television, the presence of some buffer time that removes our experience from the present occurrence makes us doubtful concerning the accuracy of the representation. The fact that our perception is never in direct contact with the present, but allows for plenty of time in which internal editing can take place, may make us similarly sceptical about the truthfulness of the representation of the world as it appears to us now.



Such scepticism is corroborated if we consider one of the more amazing tricks the brain can play with time. Once again, Libet exposed the subject to two different stimuli, one applied directly to the brain (labelled 'C' for 'cortex' in the diagram) and one applied to the skin (S). The C-stimulus was presented first, followed about 200 milliseconds later by the S-stimulus. As expected, the C-stimulus was felt after about 500 milliseconds. One would further assume that the S-stimulus is felt after 200 + 500 = 700 milliseconds. Surprisingly enough, subjects reported feeling the S-stimulus *before* the C-stimulus, after about 200 milliseconds, that is, almost immediately after it was applied to the skin.

How can this reversal of temporal ordering, which switches the true order C–S to the psychological order S–C, be explained? Of course, the S-stimulus is subject to the same half-second delay before reaching consciousness as the C-stimulus. The only explanation for this astonishing result is therefore that the brain *antedates* the onset of conscious experience of the S-stimulus from the true timing at 700 milliseconds to an apparent or subjective timing at 200 milliseconds, just after the stimulation of the skin took place. Like a TV censor switching the order of two scenes in a live broadcast, our brain is deceiving us about which event happened first. There is no guarantee that the order in which we perceive events actually corresponds to the order of their occurrence.



That our experience always lags behind the present may be regarded as an inconvenient, but not particularly important fact with few practical consequences. Yet this fact can have extremely disconcerting implications when coupled with a specific (and not unpopular view) of the reality of the three divisions of time. This is the view that only the present, but not the past or the future, is real. Presentism, as this view is known, does not just consider the present moment as experientially central, but also as ontologically central. Not only is everything we experience (sensations, memories, anticipations) experienced *now*, this 'now' is also the only thing that exists. When we talk about the past and the future, we talk about specific properties of the present (such as dinosaur bones or plans for a mission to Mars). Yet the past does not exist at all, and does not even inhabit some shadowy in-between realm between existence and non-existence. But if our perception *only* connects us with what is past, then it seems that our sense organs never manage to give us any information about the world around us. In fact, the situation is thoroughly puzzling: nothing we ever perceive exists, since everything has vanished by the time the light of our attention catches it – yet how could our entire experience, the world as we see it around us, be the perception of something non-existent?

We have seen that one part of time, namely the present, cannot be regarded as real in one of the senses of 'real' that have the most bite. The present is not apocalyptically real because in a world without minds, there would be no present moment. The present is a psychological artefact, but no constituent of a mindless world. Unless we assume that minds are an irreducible component of the world, this also implies that the present cannot be real according to the turtle definition, it cannot be one of the most fundamental constituents of the world. But what about the other parts of time, the past and the future? Even though the present has no place in physics, time has long enjoyed a very privileged position. In the Newtonian world, time is the great unifier that coordinates events everywhere in the universe. Its continuous flow from present to future determines their order and distance from each other. Yet the development of physics has since dismantled this view of time bit by bit: the 'arrow' of time, directed from the past to the future, is no longer regarded as one of its intrinsic features (but rather as a result of how matter is arranged in the universe), simultaneity depends on frames of reference, time can flow at different rates at different places, and so on.

Does physics still regard time as real according to the turtle definition, that is, as a fundamental building block of the universe, as a basic component of existence independent of anything else? Even though the fundamental timelessness of the world is hardly a matter of universal agreement amongst researchers, a number of interesting theories have been proposed that do not assume that time exists at the bottom level of reality. To see one way of arguing for this position, it is instructive to compare time with money. Nobody regards money as a fundamental constituent of the world. It is simply a device invented to make economic transactions easier. Nevertheless, such transactions are possible without money, as the example of barter economies attests. In the same way, the key function of time, to describe change, can still be carried out without any reference to time, simply by relating repeating physical processes directly to each other. Instead of saying that a bee flaps its wings 230 times per second, that a human heart beats 75 times per minute, or that the earth revolves once a day, we can describe the speed of a heart beating as 184 flaps, that of one rotation of the earth as 108,000 heartbeats, or that of one flap of a bee's wings as 0.005 heartbeats. Under these new descriptions, all references to seconds, minutes, and days have disappeared. This new way of talking about time is cumbersome, in the same way that barter economies are cumbersome. To get that clay pot you would like to have, you have to carry with you a variety of goods, hoping that the potter likes one of them enough to give you the pot in exchange. How much simpler it is to carry a neutral value-storage device called 'money' that works in a variety of situations. Similarly, how much simpler is it to have a neutral change-determining device called 'time' that can absolve you from having to measure each change in terms of some specific periodic process, such as the rotation of the earth. The proponents of a timeless world argue that our mistake is to elevate creatures of convenience like money and time to the level of real objects according to the apocalyptic or the turtle definition.

While, according to this view, time is not fundamentally real, the fact that things change is not called into doubt. We find a more radical denial of the existence of time in recent developments within physics. It is easiest to understand the fundamental concepts involved by considering a variant of the now familiar Block Universe view. Imagine a pack of playing cards and a paper-eating beetle that bores a winding tunnel through the whole pack, starting at the top card and coming out at the bottom. If we scatter the cards in the pack, it is later possible to reconstruct their original order by putting them together in such a way as to form the original tunnel. This is very much the common view of the

Block Universe, with the playing cards corresponding to the successive *nows*, and the tunnel representing the motion of an object in two-dimensional space.

Now imagine a vastly greater pack of playing cards, such that for each possible place in which a card could have a hole, there is a card which has a hole in just this place. Moreover, cards can be repeated. There may be two cards having a hole in one place, and ten million other cards having a hole in a different place. History, according to the familiar Block Universe theory, consists of adjacent playing cards with holes in very similar locations. According to the new theory, successive cards do not have to have this feature. Successive cards can have their holes in radically different places. While there is no flow of time in any kind of Block Universe theory, the familiar one at least gives us the impression of a unique series of states that constitutes history. Could we step out of time, we would see a smooth curve through the set of moments, corresponding to the changes an object undergoes in time. But according to the variant account, we cannot even have something like this static three-dimensional equivalent to change in a two-dimensional world. Reality is considerably more strange than this.



The playing cards in a pack correspond to possible states of the entire universe at a single instant. Just as cards with holes in very different places can be placed next to each other in a pack, so successive stages of the universe in time can consist of unrelated tokens of alternative states. While the usual view of the Block Universe assumes that different neighbouring stages are similar to each other in various ways, this is not the case in the variant account. The course of history is able to jump arbitrarily in the space of different alternative versions of the universe.

But how can it then be the case that we have the appearance of a smoothly changing world, where the present is very much like the recent past? We see a rolling billiard ball and therefore assume that in the previous instant the universe was such that the previous version of the ball was a little bit to the left of where we see it now. But it could be the case that the previous instant of the universe had been radically different. It does not appear to us as such because certain features in the present give the impression as if the previous moment was a particular way. And there is no other way of achieving knowledge of the past moment, for all we can do is look at certain features or structures in the present, and *infer* from these what the previous moment might have been like.

To get a bit more concrete, consider we freeze an observer's brain while he is watching a billiard ball move. The brain will encode information of the ball's present location, but also some information about the ball's previous location from earlier moments of neuronal processing. In this way, various stills are present in the brain at the same time, and the brain produces the appearance of the moving ball from the presence of simultaneous images of a stationary ball. All of this would still be possible *even if the previous moment of the universe contained no ball at all.* We can achieve the appearance of change embedded in a flowing time, and the experience of a smoothly changing history even in a world where unconnected versions of the history of the universe succeed each other in haphazard fashion. The nature of our experience of time and change therefore cannot provide an argument against the possibility of this particular variant of the Block Universe theory.

We are now ready for the final turn of the screw. Instead of saying that there is a 'smooth' passage through the different versions of the universe in the familiar Block Universe theory, or a jumpy and haphazard one in the variant just discussed, we can just say that there is *no* passage through the versions, smooth or jumpy. All the possible instantaneous configurations of the universe are equally real. Unlike in a Block Universe theory, objects in time cannot be equated with trajectories in a block. And unlike in presentist theories, there is not just one real now. All the nows are equally real, existing once and for all in some abstract, atemporal realm. We have the impression of living in a world with a past because certain structures in the now we inhabit can be interpreted as traces of previous nows that have preceded our own. It contains features that can be interpreted as mutually consistent records of processes that happened in the past in accordance with specific laws of nature.

The words 'can be interpreted' are crucial here, since there is no preceding now. If God created the world in 4004 BC, including all the fossil records, we could interpret these as evidence of animals living at much earlier times, but we would of course be mistaken. As a matter of fact, the situation is slightly more comforting in the present case, since if all the different versions of the universe are equally real, the now with the dinosaurs in it is as real as the now we are in. We can regard our now as containing a partial representation of the dinosaur-now (via the fossil records), and our claims about the existence of dinosaurs would not be wholly wrong. Dinosaurs do exist, the now they inhabit is just not the temporal predecessor of the now we are in. In this version of hyper-presentism, time is not real in any of the fundamental senses of 'real' mentioned earlier. At the most fundamental level, the world is completely static.

# Concluding remarks

Books on philosophy tend to end with a summary of the positions the author hopes to have established. I will not do this here. While the preceding pages contain a number of arguments for the unreality of things usually regarded as real (material objects, yourself, the present moment), as well as some for the reality of things often regarded as unreal (such as the future), we cannot claim that the reality or unreality of any particular things has thereby been established conclusively. To do so would take space far beyond the confines of an introductory book such as this. Just one of the issues raised here, that of the reality of the self, has been debated in the Indian philosophical tradition for at least 2,500 years and has also generated a considerable amount of philosophical literature in the West. All I could do in the preceding pages is to outline some of the major arguments in play, and give you some pointers that will enable you to continue thinking about these problems for yourself.

Instead of presenting a summary of results, what I want to do here is to introduce you to a couple of philosophical maps that make it easier to see how the various views mentioned in this book can be put together to form a coherent philosophical position. The maps consist of octagonal and square shapes, put together in a way reminiscent of the tiling on a bathroom floor. The octagons represent conscious minds, the central octagon in particular will

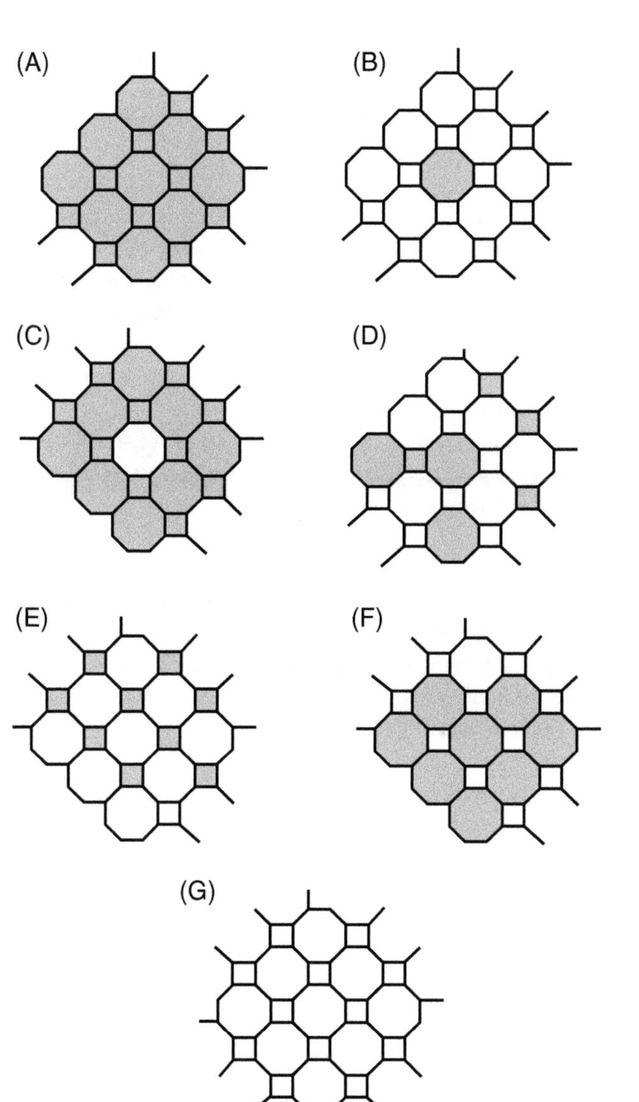


**18. Philosophical maps**

represent *you*. The squares represent all sorts of other, non-conscious things. We colour a shape grey if the object it stands for is real, otherwise we leave it white. Here are what the most important philosophical positions look like:

Map A has all the shapes coloured grey. According to this theory, which we might call *universalism*, everything is real. Electrons, minds, money, numbers are all full members of this world. The difficulty with universalism is that it will also have to regard some not so straightforward things as real, such as your non-existent twin brother or the present king of Nepal. While we might accommodate these in a realm of merely possible objects, what are we supposed to say about impossible objects, such as the largest number, the son of a barren woman, or a counterexample to Fermat's last theorem?

In comparison to this ontological jungle, map B is a lot more minimalist. The only real thing is you, and nothing else. This view, *solipsism*, has been the *femme fatale* and *bête noire* of philosophical theorizing for centuries, seductive because it appears irrefutable, frightening because such a world would strike most people as claustrophobic.



It is unfortunate that this theory received so much more attention than its equally interesting cousin, *anti-solipsism*, shown in map C. According to anti-solipsism, everything else is real, but you are not. It represents the view a fictional character might have of the world of its author (not of the fictional world he inhabits) and stands in flat opposition to our cherished belief that we are the centre of our world, the fixed point around which the great wheel of being keeps turning.

Map D represents a theory (or rather a set of theories) we might want to call *selective realism*. The majority of philosophical theories currently discussed can be subsumed under this label. According to this view, you are real, as well as a variety of other people. Not all of them are, though, characters like Lara Croft and Sherlock Holmes providing counterexamples. Of the non-conscious things represented by squares, some are real and some are not. What exactly is taken as real and what is not reflects the variety of the different theories collected together under the label 'selective realism'. For some theories, electrons might be real, and mathematical objects like numbers and functions are not. For others, mathematical objects are real, but material objects are not. For some, time is real; for some, it is not.

Despite this variety, we can make out two big subclasses amongst all the selective realisms. These are represented in maps E and F. For the first kind of theories (which I will call *mindless* theories), nothing conscious is real. At the bottom level, the world consists of things like subatomic particles, space-time points, or mathematical objects, but not of minds, persons, or selves. Such theories will of course have to explain how conscious things can arise in a mindless world. Even though mindless theories have yielded a considerable amount of insight into the relation between the mental and the physical, it is fair to say that this project has not yet been completed to everybody's satisfaction. The theories in map F, on the other hand (I call them *group-mind* theories), hold that the *only* real things are conscious things. Everything that is real is a mind, or what a mind does. The challenge is then to explain how apparently non-mental things, such as a teacup or Mount Everest, could be regarded as part of the world we live in. Instead of explaining how mind arises from matter, group-mind theories have to show how matter comes from mind.

In the final map, G, every shape is white. Nothing is real according to this theory. This admittedly very minimalist theory (called *irrealism*) fares a bit better than its close cousin nihilism, which claims that nothing exists. There are certain doubts about whether this view can even be coherently stated, for if nothing exists, then it is presumably true that nothing exists, so there is the truth that nothing exists, so there is at least one thing, namely that truth.

So something exists, which contradicts our initial assumption that nothing does. But irrealism does not face this problem. Indeed, if we understand real according to the turtle definition, it is perfectly conceivable that nothing is real, since nothing grounds the descending chain of dependence relations (either because this goes on forever, or because it forms a big loop). If irrealism is true, the *Very Short Introduction to Reality* could be a lot shorter than it actually is, since like 'Snakes in Ireland', 'Assyrio-Babylonian Philately', or 'The History of the Wheel in Pre-Columbian America', 'Reality' is a heading under which nothing falls.

# References and further reading

## Chapter 1

The series of false awakenings is described by Yves Delage in his *Le Rêve, Étude psychologique, philosophique, et littéraire*, Paris, 1923. The idea of dreams-within-dreams is intelligently applied in Christopher Nolan's 2010 film *Inception* featuring four (or five?) stacked levels of dreams.

You can calculate your own risk of death using Carnegie Mellon's death calculator at www.deathriskrankings.com.

The story of Muhammad's pitcher is referred to in part 2, chapter 5 of Dostoevsky's *The Idiot*. More information on testing the duration of dream time can be found in Stephen LaBerge, 'Lucid Dreaming: Evidence and Methodology', *Behavioral and Brain Sciences*, 23(6) (2000): 962–3. The same author's *Lucid Dreaming* (Ballantine, 1985) is a more popular treatment of various aspects of lucid dreaming.

How to keep the brains of guinea-pigs alive in a jar is described in M. Mühlethaler, M. de Curtis, K. Walton, and R. Llinás, 'The Isolated and Perfused Brain of the Guinea-Pig in Vitro', *European Journal of Neuroscience*, 5(7) (2006): 915–26.

For information on brain–computer interfaces, see Steven Kotler, 'Vision Quest', *Wired Magazine*, September 2002, pp. 94–101, and Miguel Nicolelis and John Chapin, 'Controlling Robots with the Mind', *Scientific American*, 287(4) (October 2002): 46–53.

Some discussion of the computational power of the human brain is in Nick Bostrom's 'How Long Before Superintelligence?', *Linguistic and Philosophical Investigations*, 5(1) (2006): 11–30. An updated version can be found at http://www.nickbostrom.com/superintelligence.html.

The miraculous portrait of Dean Liddell (as well as a variety of similarly spontaneously appearing portraits) is described in chapter 18 of Charles Fort's *Wild Talents* (Claude Kendall, 1932).

The main argument against the possibility of us being artificially stimulated brains goes back to Hilary Putnam's discussion in *Reason, Truth, and History* (Cambridge University Press, 1981). Since then, a vast amount of philosophical literature dealing with this argument has been written. A good first point of entry is David Chalmers's paper 'The Matrix as Metaphysics' at http://consc.net/papers/matrix.html.

For Jorge Luis Borges's story 'The Circular Ruins', see his *Collected Fictions* (Penguin, 1999), pp. 96–100.

For a quirky brief statement of anti-solipsism, see Robert Nozick's 'Fiction', chapter 19 of his *Socratic Puzzles* (Harvard University Press, 1997), pp. 313–16.

An accessible introduction to cellular automata is William Poundstone's *The Recursive Universe* (William Morrow, 1984). For a popular survey of the use of simulations in science more generally, see John L. Casti, *Would-Be Worlds: How Simulation Is Changing the Frontiers of Science* (Wiley, 1997).

For a discussion of whether we are living in a historical simulation, see Nick Bostrom, 'Are You Living in a Computer Simulation?', *Philosophical Quarterly*, 53(211) (2003): 243–55. The author also runs a website at http://www.simulation-argument.com where this paper, as well as a variety of synopses and responses are available.

The computer scientist Robert Bradbury argues that we will be able to build a Matrioshka brain, a planet-sized supercomputer that can carry out up to $10^{42}$ computational operations per second within the next century. (More information on Matrioshka brains is at http://www.aeiveos.com/~bradbury/MatrioshkaBrains.) Bostrom (247) argues that we need considerably fewer, namely a maximum of $10^{36}$ operations, to run historical simulations. The Astronomer Royal Martin Rees claims that mankind has a 50% chance of not being destroyed before the year 2100: *Our Final Century? Will the Human Race Survive the Twenty-First Century?* (Heinemann, 2003).

For more information about Zhuangzi, see Angus C. Graham (tr.), *Chuang-tzu: The Seven Inner Chapters and Other Writings from the Book Chuang-tzu* (Allen & Unwin, 1981). A translation of the butterfly dream story is on p. 61.

An analysis of the geometry underlying Escher's print is provided in chapter 6 of Bruno Ernst's *The Magic Mirror of M. C. Escher* (Taschen, 2007).

## Chapter 2

*The Matrix* gave rise to a series of books on popular philosophy of variable quality. One of the better ones is William Irwin (ed.), *The Matrix and Philosophy* (Open Court, 2002).

The quotation from George Orwell's *Nineteen Eighty-Four* is in chapter 2 of part 3 (p. 249 of the Penguin edition).

For some discussion of Koro, see B. Y. Ng, 'History of Koro in Singapore', *Singapore Medical Journal*, 38(8) (August 1969): 356–7. A more general study of mass hallucinations is Robert E. Bartholomew's *Meowing Nuns and Head-Hunting Panics: A Study of Mass Psychogenic Illnesses and Social Delusion* (McFarland, 2001); chapter 8 deals specifically with Koro.

James Boswell relates Dr Johnson's reaction to Berkeley in volume 1 of his *Life of Johnson*, edited by George Birckbeck (Hill, Bigelow, Brown, 1921), p. 545. From a philosophical point of view, Johnson's reply is woefully inadequate (nowhere does Berkeley claim that the mental nature of rocks and stones entails that they stop being hard), even though it does not lack a certain rustic charm. For what Berkeley would have replied, see his *Principles of Human Knowledge and Three Dialogues*, edited by Howard Robinson (Oxford University Press, 1996), p. 129. A more sophisticated variant of Johnson's definition is given in chapter 4 of David Deutsch's *The Fabric of Reality* (Penguin, 1997).

The quotation from Philip K. Dick comes from his 'How to Build a Universe That Doesn't Fall Apart Two Days Later', in *The Shifting Realities of Philip K. Dick: Selected Literary and Philosophical Writings* (Vintage, 1996), pp. 259–80.

An interesting exploration of how the world would develop if all human beings suddenly vanished is presented by Alan Weisman in *The World Without Us* (Virgin Books, 2008).

The quotation from Locke's *An Essay Concerning Human Understanding* can be found on pp. 391–2 of the first volume of the Dover edition (New York, 1959). It is hard to find the Indian source of the cosmological theory that the earth rests on an elephant and this on a tortoise (and the tortoise perhaps on something unknown, or nothing at all, or most intriguing, on a downwards infinite column of further tortoises). The earliest mention of this theory traceable so far comes from a letter written by a Jesuit missionary in India in 1599. Up to now, I have not been able to find any Indian text describing a stacked elephant-tortoise support.

A clear discussion of Vasubandhu's arguments about the reality of matter is in Matthew Kapstein's 'Mereological Considerations in Vasubandhu's "Proof of Idealism"' reprinted in his *Reason's Traces* (Wisdom, 2001), pp. 181–204. The same issues are taken up later in Immanuel Kant's so-called second antinomy, on which see James van Cleve, 'Reflections on Kant's Second Antinomy', *Synthese*, 47(3) (1981): 481–94.

The best introduction to Berkeley's thought is still his very lively set of *Three Dialogues Between Hylas and Philonous*. See George Berkeley, *Principles of Human Knowledge and Three Dialogues*, edited by Howard Robinson (Oxford University Press, 1996), pp. 97–208.

A tear-free introduction to key quantum mechanical concepts and a clear comparison of the various interpretations of the quantum mechanical formalism can be found in Nick Herbert's *Quantum Reality* (Doubleday, 1985). A highly readable set of interviews with some of the key players in the development of quantum physics (originally produced as a BBC Radio 3 documentary) is P. C. W. Davies and J. R. Brown's *The Ghost in the Atom* (Cambridge University Press, 1986).

For an account of the buckyball, see Markus Arndt et al., 'Wave–Particle Duality of C60 Molecules', *Nature*, 401 (1999): 680–2.

The experiment involving the metal strip is described in A. D. O'Connell et al., 'Quantum Ground State and Single-Phonon Control of a Mechanical Resonator', *Nature*, 464 (2010): 697–703.

Eugene Wigner's remarks on the role of consciousness in quantum measurement can be found in his 'Remarks on the Mind–Body Question', included in a collection of essays entitled *Symmetries and Reflections* (Indiana University Press, 1967), pp. 171–84. More details on the case of 'Wigner's friend', an interesting variant of the thought experiment involving Schrödinger's cat, can be found in chapter 7 of Paul Davies, *Other Worlds: Space, Superspace and the Quantum Universe* (Simon & Schuster, 1980). For more recent developments arguing for the observer-dependence of what is real, see Matteo Smerlak and Carlo Rovelli, 'Relational EPR', http://xxx.lanl.gov/abs/quant-ph/0604064.

Roger Penrose describes his theories on the role of quantum phenomena in the explanation of consciousness in his *Shadows of the Mind: A Search for the Missing Science of Consciousness* (Oxford University Press, 1994).

The quotation from Werner Heisenberg comes from his *Physics and Philosophy* (Harper & Row, 1962), p. 145.

Some more thoughts on scientific reduction can be found in W. V. Quine's 'Things and Their Place in Theories', in his *Theories and Things* (Harvard University Press, 1981).

Stewart Shapiro's *Thinking about Mathematics* (Oxford University Press, 2000) provides an accessible introduction to the Platonic view of mathematical objects, as well as to a variety of other theories of the nature of mathematics.

For a popular yet comprehensive account of theories that conceive of the physical world as the output of a computational process, see Kevin Kelly's 'God Is the Machine', *Wired*, 10(12) (2002).

For Bohr's view of the non-existence of quantum objects, see the discussion in Max Jammer's *The Philosophy of Quantum Mechanics* (Wiley, 1974), pp. 203–11. This is an excellent if demanding resource for analyses of the key aspects of the interpretation of the quantum mechanical formalism.



## Chapter 3

The curious experiences of the woman who irretrievably lost her self are described in Suzanne Segal's very readable memoir *Collision with the Infinite: A Life Beyond the Personal Self* (Blue Dove Press, 1998). For more information on Cotard's syndrome, see chapter 8 of David Enoch and Adrian Ball, *Uncommon Psychiatric Syndromes* (Hodder & Stoughton, 2001).

For an overview of the different locations of the self throughout history, see Giuseppe Santoro et al., 'The Anatomic Location of the Soul From the Heart, Through the Brain, To the Whole Body, and Beyond', *Neurosurgery*, 65(4) (2009): 633–43.

Daniel Dennett's 'Where Am I?' is reprinted in chapter 13 of the excellent anthology *The Mind's I*, edited by Douglas Hofstadter and Daniel Dennett (Harvester Press, 1981). The selection given here is on pp. 218–19. In 1988, the Dutch director Piet Hoenderdos turned Dennett's story into a film (starring Daniel Dennett as Daniel Dennett). You can watch it at <http://video.google.com/videoplay?docid=8576072297424860224#>

The experiment with the virtual full-body illusion is described in Thomas Metzinger's *The Ego Tunnel: The Science of the Mind and the Myth of the Self* (Basic Books, 2009), pp. 98–101.

A variant of the thought experiment of the self-destroying drug is described in Raymond Smullyan's essay 'An Unfortunate Dualist' in his *This Book Needs No Title* (Simon & Schuster, 1980), pp. 53–5. This piece is discussed in *The Mind's I*, pp. 384–8, where the original essay is also reprinted.

The quote from David Hume comes from his *Treatise of Human Nature* (Clarendon Press, 1896), p. 252.

The quote from Descartes can be found in John Cottingham et al., *The Philosophical Writings of Descartes*, Vol. III: *The Correspondence* (Cambridge University Press, 1991), p. 143.

For more on the total flight simulator, see Thomas Metzinger's *The Ego Tunnel: The Science of the Mind and the Myth of the Self* (Basic Books, 2009), pp. 104–8.

For the text of the entire *Mahāpuṇṇama Sutta*, see Bikkhu Ñāṇamoli and Bikkhu Bodhi (tr.), *The Middle Length Discourses of the Buddha* (Wisdom, 1995), pp. 887–91. For a related view of the self, see Derek Parfit's *Reasons and Persons* (Clarendon Press, 1984).

Jorge Luis Borges describes the work of Tsu'i Pen in his story 'The Garden of Forking Paths'. See his *Collected Fictions* (Penguin, 1999), pp. 119–28.

Accessible introductions to the many worlds interpretation are in Nick Herbert's *Quantum Reality* (Doubleday, 1985), pp. 172–5, and Paul Davies's *Other Worlds* (Simon & Schuster, 1980). For an interesting discussion that seeks to dispel some of the philosophical perplexities generated by this interpretation, see chapter 13 of Michael Lockwood's *Mind, Brain and Quantum* (Basil Blackwell, 1989).

For Libet's experiments, see Benjamin Libet et al., 'Time of Conscious Intention to Act in Relation to Onset of Cerebral Activity (Readiness Potential): The Unconscious Initiation of a Freely Voluntary Act', *Brain*, 106(3) (1983): 623–42.

Information on the influence of transcranial magnetic stimulation on intentional choice can be found in Joaquim Brasil-Neto et al., 'Focal Transcranial Magnetic Stimulation and Response Bias in a Forced-Choice Task', *Journal of Neurology, Neurosurgery, and Psychiatry*, 55 (1992): 964–6.

The experiment with the shared computer mouse is described in Daniel Wegner and Thalia Wheatley, 'Apparent Mental Causation:

Sources of the Experience of Will', *American Psychologist*, 54 (1999): 480–92. Further discussion is in Daniel Wegner's 'The Mind's Best Trick: How We Experience Conscious Will', *Trends in Cognitive Sciences*, 7(2) (2003): 65–9, and Thomas Metzinger's *The Ego Tunnel: The Science of the Mind and the Myth of the Self* (Basic Books, 2009), pp. 122–6.

Memetics was introduced by Richard Dawkins in his 1976 book *The Selfish Gene*, which popularized the idea of gene-centred (rather than organism-centred) evolution. For more information on the t-gene in mice, see p. 236 of the thirtieth anniversary edition (Oxford, 2006). The view of the relation between memes and the self is set forth in Daniel Dennett's *Consciousness Explained* (Penguin, 1993), pp. 199–208. A book-length discussion arriving at similar conclusions is Susan Blackmore's *The Meme Machine* (Oxford University Press, 1999). For a different interpretation, see Kate Distin's *The Selfish Meme: A Critical Reassessment* (Cambridge University Press, 2005).

## Chapter 4

The legend of the monk of Heisterbach is told in Goswin Peter Rath's *Rheinische Legenden* (Greven Verlag Cologne, 1955), pp. 178–81.

McTaggart describes his proof of the unreality of time first in a paper of the same title in volume 17 of *Mind* (1908: 457–74), and later in chapter 33 of his two-volume *The Nature of Existence* (Cambridge University Press, 1921). An accessible summary of the argument can be found in chapter 8 of Robin Le Poidevin's *Travels in Four Dimensions: The Enigmas of Space and Time* (Oxford University Press, 2003). McTaggart's argument has triggered a large amount of philosophical discussion; the Further Reading in this volume lists the most important contributions.

A clear discussion of Gödel's thought on time can be found in Palle Yourgrau's *Gödel Meets Einstein* (Open Court, 1999). For an excellent explanation of the relativity of simultaneity, see Martin Gardner's *Relativity for the Million* (Macmillan, 1962), pp. 40–5.

Russell's five-minute hypothesis comes from his *The Analysis of Mind* (Allen & Unwin, 1921), p. 159. A similar argument is used by creationists to explain the existence of objects apparently pre-dating their preferred date of creation: God, it is claimed, just created all the apparent records of an illusory past at the same time as everything else. For some discussion, see chapter 1 of Martin Gardner's *Did Adam and Eve Have Navels?* (W. W. Norton, 2000).

Felix Eberty first describes his idea of the present universe as a massive visual archive of the past in a short anonymous pamphlet *Die Gestirne und die Weltgeschichte; Gedanken über Raum, Zeit und Ewigkeit* published in 1846. It was further developed by Harry Mulisch in his 1997 novel *The Discovery of Heaven*: 'If we had the technology to place a mirror on a celestial object forty light-years away, beamed images from earth to that mirror, then gazed at it through a very powerful telescope, we would see right now reflections of what took place on earth eighty years ago – forty years for earth's light to reach the distant planet, and forty years for the reflection to reach earth. Past and present merge.'

On the phantom time hypothesis, see Heribert Illig, *Das erfundene Mittelalter. Die größte Zeitfälschung der Geschichte* (Econ, 1996). Material in English is limited, a summary can be found in Hans-Ulrich Niemitz's 'Did the Early Middle Ages Really Exist?', at http://www.cl.cam.ac.uk/~mgk25/volatile/Niemitz-1997.pdf. For a brief discussion, see also John Grant's *Bogus Science* (Wisley, 2009), pp. 179–85.

For an accessible summary of the delayed-choice experiment, see Nick Herbert's *Quantum Reality* (Doubleday, 1985), pp. 164–8. You can do your own delayed-choice experiment at home by following the description in Rachel Hillmer and Paul Kwiat, 'A Do-It-Yourself Quantum Eraser', *Scientific American* (May 2007): 90–5.

The name 'Andromeda paradox' derives from the discussion by Roger Penrose in his *The Emperor's New Mind* (Oxford University Press, 1999), pp. 260–1. The paradox had previously been discovered independently by C. W. Rietdijk in 'A Rigorous Proof of Determinism Derived from the Special Theory of Relativity', *Philosophy of Science*, 33 (1966): 341–4, and by Hilary Putnam in 'Time and Physical Geometry', *Journal of Philosophy*, 64 (1967): 240–4. For a detailed analysis of this paradox, see section 3 of the entry 'Being and Becoming in Modern Physics' in the *Stanford Encyclopedia of Philosophy* at <http://plato.stanford.edu/entries/spacetime-bebecome>.

The extract from the *Confessions* of St Augustine comes from section 26 of the eleventh book, E. B. Pusey (tr.), *The Confessions of S. Augustine* (John Henry Parker, 1838), p. 239.

For research into the duration of the subjective present, see Ernst Pöppel, *Mindworks: Time and Conscious Experience* (Harcourt Brace Jovanovich, 1988).

For some discussion of how the brain represents time, see pp. 144–53 of Daniel Dennett's *Consciousness Explained* (Penguin, 1991).

A description of Libet's experiments aimed at a general readership can be found in chapter 2 of his *Mind Time: The Temporal Factor in Consciousness* (Harvard University Press, 2004).

The 'timeless' theory described at the end of the chapter is due to Julian Barbour and is explained in detail in his book *The End of Time: The Next Revolution in Our Understanding of the Universe* (Phoenix, 1999). A highly informative review of this book and a discussion of many related issues by Jeremy Butterfield was published in the *British Journal for the Philosophy of Science*, 53 (2002): 289–330. An extended version of this piece is available at <http://arxiv.org/abs/gr-qc/0103055>.

# Publisher's acknowledgements

Excerpt on p.18 from "The Circular Ruins" by Jorge Luis Borges, translated by James E. Irby, from LABYRINTHS, copyright © 1962, 1964, by New Directions Publishing Corp. Reprinted by permission of New Directions Publishing Corp and Pollinger Limited.

Excerpt on p.61 from Dennett's *Where Am I*? reproduced from Daniel C. Dennett, BRAINSTORMS: PHILOSOPHICAL ESSAYS ON MIND AND PSYCHOLOGY, ©MIT 1981, by permission of The MIT Press.

# Index

# PHILOSOPHY

## A Very Short Introduction

Edward Craig

This lively and engaging book is the ideal introduction for anyone who has ever been puzzled by what philosophy is or what it is for.

Edward Craig argues that philosophy is not an activity from another planet: learning about it is just a matter of broadening and deepening what most of us do already. He shows that philosophy is no mere intellectual pastime: thinkers such as Plato, Buddhist writers, Descartes, Hobbes, Hume, Hegel, Darwin, Mill and de Beauvoir were responding to real needs and events – much of their work shapes our lives today, and many of their concerns are still ours.

'A vigorous and engaging introduction that speaks to the philosopher in everyone.'

**John Cottingham, University of Reading**

'addresses many of the central philosophical questions in an engaging and thought-provoking style . . . Edward Craig is already famous as the editor of the best long work on philosophy (the Routledge Encyclopedia); now he deserves to become even better known as the author of one of the best short ones.'

**Nigel Warburton, The Open University**

www.oup.com/vsi/

# NUMBERS

## A Very Short Introduction

Peter M. Higgins

Numbers are integral to our everyday lives and feature in everything we do. In this *Very Short Introduction* Peter M. Higgins, the renowned mathematics writer unravels the world of numbers; demonstrating its richness, and providing a comprehensive view of the idea of the number. Higgins paints a picture of the number world, considering how the modern number system matured over centuries. Explaining the various number types and showing how they behave, he introduces key concepts such as integers, fractions, real numbers, and imaginary numbers. By approaching the topic in a non-technical way and emphasising the basic principles and interactions of numbers with mathematics and science, Higgins also demonstrates the practical interactions and modern applications, such as encryption of confidential data on the internet.

www.oup.com/vsi

# NOTHING

## A Very Short Introduction

Frank Close

What is 'nothing'? What remains when you take all the matter away? Can empty space - a void - exist? This *Very Short Introduction* explores the science and history of the elusive void: from Aristotle's theories to black holes and quantum particles, and why the latest discoveries about the vacuum tell us extraordinary things about the cosmos. Frank Close tells the story of how scientists have explored the elusive void, and the rich discoveries that they have made there. He takes the reader on a lively and accessible history through ancient ideas and cultural superstitions to the frontiers of current research.

> 'An accessible and entertaining read for layperson and scientist alike.'
>
> Physics World

www.oup.com/vsi

# INFORMATION
## A Very Short Introduction
Luciano Floridi

Luciano Floridi, a philosopher of information, cuts across many subjects, from a brief look at the mathematical roots of information - its definition and measurement in 'bits'- to its role in genetics (we are information), and its social meaning and value. He ends by considering the ethics of information, including issues of ownership, privacy, and accessibility; copyright and open source. For those unfamiliar with its precise meaning and wide applicability as a philosophical concept, 'information' may seem a bland or mundane topic. Those who have studied some science or philosophy or sociology will already be aware of its centrality and richness. But for all readers, whether from the humanities or sciences, Floridi gives a fascinating and inspirational introduction to this most fundamental of ideas.

'Splendidly pellucid.'

**Steven Poole, The Guardian**

www.oup.com/vsi

# GALAXIES

## A Very Short Introduction

John Gribbin

Galaxies are the building blocks of the Universe: standing like islands in space, each is made up of many hundreds of millions of stars in which the chemical elements are made, around which planets form, and where on at least one of those planets intelligent life has emerged. In this *Very Short Introduction*, renowned science writer John Gribbin describes the extraordinary things that astronomers are learning about galaxies, and explains how this can shed light on the origins and structure of the Universe.

www.oup.com/vsi

# Existentialism

## A Very Short Introduction

Thomas Flynn

Existentialism was one of the leading philosophical movements of the twentieth century. Focusing on its seven leading figures, Sartre, Nietzsche, Heidegger, Kierkegaard, de Beauvoir, Merleau-Ponty and Camus, this *Very Short Introduction* provides a clear account of the key themes of the movement which emphasized individuality, free will, and personal responsibility in the modern world. Drawing in the movement's varied relationships with the arts, humanism, and politics, this book clarifies the philosophy and original meaning of 'existentialism' - which has tended to be obscured by misappropriation. Placing it in its historical context, Thomas Flynn also highlights how existentialism is still relevant to us today.

www.oup.com/vsi

# CRITICAL THEORY

## A Very Short Introduction

Stephen Eric Bronner

In its essence, Critical Theory is Western Marxist thought with the emphasis moved from the liberation of the working class to broader issues of individual agency. Critical Theory emerged in the 1920s from the work of the Frankfurt School, the circle of German-Jewish academics who sought to diagnose--and, if at all possible, cure--the ills of society, particularly fascism and capitalism.  In this book, Stephen Eric Bronner provides sketches of famous and less famous representatives of the critical tradition (such as George Lukács and Ernst Bloch, Theodor Adorno and Walter Benjamin, Herbert Marcuse and Jurgen Habermas) as well as many of its seminal texts and empirical investigations.

www.oup.com/vsi

# Conscience
# A Very Short Introduction

Paul Strohm

In the West conscience has been relied upon for two thousand years as a judgement that distinguishes right from wrong. It has effortlessly moved through every period division and timeline between the ancient, medieval, and modern. The Romans identified it, the early Christians appropriated it, and Reformation Protestants and loyal Catholics relied upon its advice and admonition. Today it is embraced with equal conviction by non-religious and religious alike. Considering its deep historical roots and exploring what it has meant to successive generations, Paul Strohm highlights why this particularly European concept deserves its reputation as 'one of the prouder Western contributions to human rights and human dignity throughout the world.

www.oup.com/vsi

# CHAOS

## A Very Short Introduction

Leonard Smith

Our growing understanding of Chaos Theory is having fascinating applications in the real world - from technology to global warming, politics, human behaviour, and even gambling on the stock market. Leonard Smith shows that we all have an intuitive understanding of chaotic systems. He uses accessible maths and physics (replacing complex equations with simple examples like pendulums, railway lines, and tossing coins) to explain the theory, and points to numerous examples in philosophy and literature (Edgar Allen Poe, Chang-Tzu, Arthur Conan Doyle) that illuminate the problems. The beauty of fractal patterns and their relation to chaos, as well as the history of chaos, and its uses in the real world and implications for the philosophy of science are all discussed in this *Very Short Introduction*.

> '. . . Chaos . . . will give you the clearest (but not too painful idea) of the maths involved . . . There's a lot packed into this little book, and for such a technical exploration it's surprisingly readable and enjoyable - I really wanted to keep turning the pages. Smith also has some excellent words of wisdom about common misunderstandings of chaos theory . . .'
>
> **popularscience.co.uk**

www.oup.com/vsi